HOW TO HEAL TOXIC THOUGHTS

RACHEL STONE

Hackney and Jones

HACKNEY & JONES

Claim Your Freebie NOW!

Get Good At Problem Solving

Want to know the secret behind getting good at problem solving? Everyone seems to be able to do it, but you're stuck in the pile of endless to-do lists with little progress.

Ok, so how do I get my FREE book?

EASY! See the next page

Claim Your Freebie NOW

Instructions:

1. Open the camera or the QR reader application on your smartphone.
2. Point your camera at the QR code to scan the QR code.
3. A notification will pop-up on screen.
4. Click on the notification to open the website link

Also By Rachel Stone

How To Remove Negativity From Your Life

Rid yourself forever from the negative thoughts that plague your life with this amazing, life-changing book.

Also By Rachel Stone

Start Being Fearless, Stop Being Scared

Fed up of being scared of the things in life that hold you back? It's time to take control back and start being fearless.

Also By Rachel Stone

Why Living a Simple Life is Better for You

An easy guide to help you change the way you think about your life. Take steps to start living a stress-free life.

Grab the Rachel Stone series NOW

Instructions:

1. Open the camera or the QR reader application on your smartphone.
2. Point your camera at the QR code to scan the QR code.
3. A notification will pop-up on screen.
4. Click on the notification to open the website link

Join in!

If you would like to find out what projects we have on the go, or get in touch with us, simply click on the link below:

http://hackneyandjones.com

Contents

Introduction

We have a lot to think about these days—the money to buy everything we need, our work obligations, our kids and families... you name it. There are several reasons to be concerned about the toxic thoughts that are building up inside us. We also have a never-ending to-do list to finish this week, with deadlines every day that we may or may not reach. The problem is that we are now busier than ever before, with many more obligations than we used to have. Previous generations had much to do as well, but they also had some downtime. We're in a position where our schedules are so jam-packed that we can't sit down and relax after a while. Our bodies and brains are cluttered with stress and mental clutter, producing anxiety and melancholy. We are unable to concentrate on what has to be done, and as a result of that, we become even more anxious and frightened. Consider it a stress mountain that is forming.

You may believe that the entire world forces you to be concerned and that being worried all of the time is socially responsible and ethical. This is, however, not how you should spend your life. Instead of stressing about tomorrow, why not toss your concerns out the window? Make use of comedy to brighten you up. Stop worrying about the insignificant things that accumulate and start infusing more good energy into your life. Only then can you have more happiness and meaning in your life. It all starts with looking on the bright side of things and believing that you can attain your objectives.

This book was designed to serve as a starting point for you on your journey of self-discovery. It is a guide to help you to get out of the habit of worrying about everything. This book will assist you in overcoming your greatest anxieties and help you to live a more relaxed life, sleep better and become more carefree. Furthermore, it will assist you in overcoming the obstacles that are impeding your progress and will provide you with the confidence to deal with all of the worries and problems that may overwhelm your life.

In this book we will look at the causes of mental clutter. We'll discover how to have a good mentality, how to be proactive in your life, and how to live a life that will get you back on track. It's easy to believe that your life is out of control and that you have a lot on your mind, but hold your horses. Stop allowing your emotions to rule you and give yourself a break. That is the only way you will feel liberated. By the end of this book, you will be well on your way to eradicating toxic thoughts from your life forever.

Don't let oppression's chains lead you down a dark and unsustainable road. Instead, revel in the satisfaction of knowing that tomorrow will be fine and that life will improve. Every day will be better than the one before it, and once you realise it, you'll be happier than you've ever been, knowing that you can do your best to live a healthy life. Let us go on this trip together to overcome our greatest anxieties, worry less, and live in a prosperous and happy future.

Are you ready to heal those toxic thoughts once and for all? If you want to start living a life where you can belly laugh for the first time in ages, or actually sleep through the night then keep reading.

1

What Seems To Be The Problem?

YOU'RE THINKING about your to-do list for today, which feels overwhelming:

- Your son's soccer practice is scheduled for 7:00 p.m.
- You must complete your most recent project and may have to stay up till 2:00 a.m. to do so.
- The laundry is building up since no one has done it in two weeks, and the dishes are stacking up.

A lot of stuff is clogging up your life. Many of us have activities that generate brain congestion. Every day, we have specific mental fire drills that we have to face, making it simple to stress and fret about what we're going to do. Worrying, on the other hand, does not assist but rather aggravates the situation. The essential thing for us to focus on is how to deal with our mental clutter since that is how we will go forward in our lives. But, before we accomplish that, we need to figure out what causes us to feel anxious and have mental clutter in our lives.

Toxic thoughts encompass anything that enters our life and lead us to feel overwhelmed by our to-do list. It comprises items on our to-do list, regrets for previous actions, incomplete tasks, such as messages to send and bills to pay, among other things. We also worry about several things, even if we don't know if they will happen or not. Grumbling and whining may also be a source of mental clutter. Finally, perfectionism impairs our capacity to progress because it causes us to be concerned about things we have no control over. We try our hardest at life yet are afraid of falling short.

Procrastination

This is a huge one since it's something that many people do all the time, and it just leads to a lot of sorrow and grief. Many of us wait until the last minute to do anything, and then we feel overwhelmed by the work involved because we believe it is too tough to do in such a short period, causing a great deal of tension and worry. Then we start worrying about how we're going to get it done. Procrastination is one of the hardest things we encounter daily, but it can be prevented with appropriate preparation and organisation. However, many people fail to prioritise chores or create a timetable. As a result, they don't know what to do when they have a lot to do. One method to cope with this is to write down everything that needs to be done and then tick things off one-by-one, bit-by-bit, step-by-step. This method is informally known as "eating the elephant."

Case study

Laura's to-do list was far too long. Every day, she felt farther behind on the things she needed to accomplish because she wanted to spend more time on the things that were important to her and less time on the things that were burdening her. Furthermore, she would forget about some of the tough tasks for her, just to discover that she needed to do them. That's when she recognised she needed to shift her mentality from being a procrastinator to being proactive in transforming her life. As a result, she resolved to organise her life and prevent procrastination as much as possible. It aided her and made a significant difference in her life.

Doing Too Much, Staying Too Busy

Much of modern life is frantic and chaotic, with individuals taking on more than they can handle and becoming stressed as a result. When we add too many tasks to our to-do list, we frequently become more stressed since we are unsure how everything will be completed. However, lightening our burdens and attempting to do less can benefit our general psychology and how we think about certain circumstances. It would help if you strived to lighten your load by taking on fewer responsibilities. This will allow you to do much more and be more efficient.

Case study

Kathleen was always on the go. Her day was crammed with stuff she had to do all the time. Her lessons were from 8:00 a.m. to 3:00 p.m. She then had to attend her debate club from 3:00 to 5:00 p.m., following her classes. She would then have dinner. On Mondays, Wednesdays, and Fridays after supper, she would go to her salsa club, and then she would do homework until 2:00 or 3:00 a.m. She would then get up at 7:00 a.m. She was overburdened. She didn't know she was accomplishing a lot until her hectic schedule caught up with her. Kathleen soon began to have panic attacks and inexplicable discomfort in her side due to her nervous bouts.

Daily Tasks

Daily tension may contribute to our mental clutter and stress, from getting on the train in the morning with a swarm of people so close that you are out of your comfort zone, to your job and family life responsibilities. As a result, we must understand how to cope with them.

Some of the negative impacts of daily stress include difficulty sleeping, muscular pains, chest discomfort, and headaches. The bodily manifestations of our stress may cause us great worry, so we must keep an eye out for them. Mental tension, at its worst, may lead to marital issues, panic attacks, and despair.

. . .

Case Study

Mike was a TV news anchor who had to go to dangerous and difficult-to-report on locations like Afghanistan, Israel, and Palestine. He would drink a lot of alcohol or smoke marijuana to cope with the everyday stress of a potential on-air assault.

Mike met with his doctor, who briefed him about his mental condition. His doctor advised him to take care of his health and be careful of what he did to avoid going down the wrong path. The doctor also gave him some medicines to aid with his mood swings and anxiousness. It would allow him to execute his work more efficiently. In addition, Mike quit using recreational drugs and alcohol to cope with his stress. Instead, he took his prescription exactly as prescribed. He attempted some exercise, which also aided him.

Too Many Choices

Do you know that dreadful sensation you get when you have to make a selection in the grocery store or a restaurant? There are too many options on the menu or at the shop, and it is easy to feel overwhelmed and not know what to select. Our mental health might suffer due to our freedom of choice, as we may experience increased worry, immobility, and unhappiness with our life. Additional alternatives provide us with more possibilities, but they do not ensure our pleasure.

Consider your next trip to the store. As reported by the Food Marketing Institute, the typical supermarket had 42,214 products in 2014. What used to take no more than fifteen minutes now requires customers to spend more time determining what they want. As a result, going through the store takes at least thirty minutes. Not to add, depending on how busy the store is on any given day, it might take even longer to check out.

Go to a store and try on a pair of khaki trousers. There are several options. Do you like a roomy fit, a straight fit, a slim fit, a wide leg, or a zipper? It makes it tough to make a decision.

Too Many Things In Your Closet

Nowadays, our houses are cluttered with items we never use, such as books we never read, DVDs we never watch, devices that collect dust, and clothes we never wear. Our email inboxes are more cluttered than ever, and our phones constantly remind us that we need more storage.

As we load our houses with more items than we need, our thoughts get increasingly cluttered with worry. And then we're at a loss as to what to do with it all. We are surrounded by information, yet we don't know how to manage it all. We can order anything online, from a bicycle to cleaning supplies, with the touch of a button. We don't even need to get out of the house. But then, as we obtain more, we get more boxes, and we realise we need even more storage because we have too many supplies. It's an endless loop.

Furthermore, we must purge the items that are cluttering our life to make place for new items. You can imagine how emotionally and psychologically draining this is for you and your family. As a result, you must get rid of the garbage that is giving you so much trouble.

Case study

Richard was a slacker. He had a lot of old documents in his desk drawer, which he kept closed. But once he opened it, a slew of objects flew out all over the place. Richard had no idea how much he was putting things away. This, however, became an important element of his mental condition. He was constantly tense. He procrastinated a lot on projects and was generally disorganised. Richard's pack-rat thinking was causing him to battle on so many levels to keep his life in order, and it was tough for him to manage all of the problems that he was experiencing. Consequently, Richard would soon have to learn how to manage his life and arrange his belongings so that he wouldn't postpone or store items in his drawers and closet. He finally got rid of items and went through a "deep cleansing" procedure to get anything he didn't need out of his house. It was a beneficial procedure for him.

Every Message Must Be Answered

As our lives get more crowded, we understand that every text or email must be responded to. With our latest technologies, we are always feeling pressed for time in our lives. We are continuously ingesting new knowledge, which keeps us on our toes and prevents us from relaxing from our frantic existence. However, our bustle will drive us to a point where we are fully fatigued and unable to continue. Then we start to break down and worry about everything, keeping us up at night and leaving us in a perpetual state of misery because we're trying to keep up with our difficult existence.

Case study

Susan had become a slave to her phone. She would leave all of her alerts on, which was causing her worry and anxiety. Every time a notification appeared on her idle phone, she felt compelled to pick it up and reply immediately.

She would frequently complete all of her jobs in this manner. But then it infiltrated her life and began to distract her from the vital things she needed to accomplish. She found herself responding SMS and other work-related communications until 2:00 or 3:00 a.m. Her work-life balance was suffering, and she became ill on occasion. She eventually felt unwell and caught the flu, leaving her confined to her home for many days. Susan felt terrible and realised she had to do something to alleviate her anxiety due to her job and the continual need to be attentive to her friends, family, and coworkers. She began to turn off notifications and only checked her phone at specific times of the day. Then she realised how much more calm she felt when she didn't spend five to six hours on the phone every day but instead reduced it to two or three hours. It had a significant impact on her life.

The Tendency To React Negatively To Situations

As humans, we tend to respond adversely to events, whether we are aware of it or not. Negative responses are prevalent because they arouse negative feelings inside us, causing tension and worry, which causes us to feel depressed, angry, and dissatisfied. Consider social media. See how much negativity travels through the grapevine. People like gossiping about others and then whining about what they perceive to be wrongdoing. That is not how you should spend your life. It's such a waste to spend all of your time worrying about what other people are doing and not enough time worrying about what you're doing. However, many individuals do this daily and are unaware of how much it impacts them personally. It generates a lot of emotional and mental congestion in your head, which is unhealthy and strains your relationships with others.

Case Study

Lisa was a Negative Nelly. She came into places and complained about her job, causing other people to pick up on her negative vibe. It was intense, and it affected everyone else's emotions. Also, she liked to stir things up, and she even liked to gossip about her coworkers behind their backs to set them against each other. Lisa was unaware that she was generating mental congestion in others, but it was apparent that people were becoming upset. It was difficult for others to see the difficulties. She quickly made more than a few enemies in the workplace, and she was eventually fired for contributing to an overall unfriendly and unpleasant environment for everyone.

Emotional And Mental Baggage

Every day, we may become victims of our heartbreaks and baggage that has crept back into our lives from the past. Often, our past wounds, fears, and interpersonal difficulties have caused us so much stress. Sometimes you aren't even searching for it, but it comes back to haunt you, and you feel as if you can't bear it anymore. It makes things difficult for you. You find it difficult to do the things you want because you are so focused on the wrong things you have done in the past. This might be a hurdle that you must overcome to achieve your goals in life. That can only be accomplished by letting go of everything that is holding you back. It would be best if you let go of the past's tension, forgive those who have harmed you, and move on. That is easier said than done, but doing so will help you enhance your entire mental state and add to your overall happiness.

Case Study

Steven became a victim and, in effect, a prisoner of his past. He was continually thinking about what upset him, especially an enemy from his schooldays. He became enraged with him as he remembered a scar from his past with this guy. It prompted him to retain thoughts of unforgiveness in his heart, making him unable to interact with him. Steven finally realised he had to let it all go. This self-inflicted misery was giving him internal pain and anguish. It was turning him into a horrible guy who solely held grudges against people. He realised he needed to go away from it all. So, eventually, he confided in his childhood enemy and disclosed his grievances against him. Many times, all that is required is conversation and reconciliation to bring two broken people back together in a way that makes things better.

As you can see from all of the case studies above, mental clutter continues to have a detrimental impact on our lives. It makes us feel concerned and nervous about the things that are going on in our life. Then we feel crushed beneath the weight of everything since we don't know what to do about it all. We end up worrying about everything that needs to be done. However, there are methods for dealing with our concerns. With a little proactivity and patience with yourself, you can overcome these obstacles. The sooner you overcome, the sooner you will feel released from your internal enslavement to fear, and you will be able to live a life full of meaning and enjoyment.

. . .

Allow yourself to be liberated from all that is stifling you. You will feel better and be able to deal with any obstacle that comes your way. Release and let it all go, and you will notice a change.

You've got this!

2

Research Into Toxic Thoughts

We tend to extol our brains and focus on everything we have accomplished with them, from constructing pyramids to landing on the moon. However, our brains may also imprison us by producing tormenting impressions, ideas, and beliefs. Doubts might arise in your mind regularly, causing you to be concerned. It might take up your attention with thoughts you can't get out of your head. It might make you feel as if you have to do something repeatedly to feel relieved. It may keep you from making even the most basic decisions by continuously generating alternative scenarios, making it appear challenging to know what's correct.

The million-dollar-question is **HOW** do you break free from the processes that the brain generates?

This appears to be a difficult question to answer. Most of us are unaware of how reliant we are on our brains for our view of reality until we lose it. The way the brain functions shapes our perceptions, with several areas of the brain contributing to each impression.

. . .

Case study

Melissa was hit by a car and banged her head on the pavement, causing injury to the fusiform gyrus at the rear of her brain. She found herself unable to identify faces for the first time. She saw someone's face, but she couldn't determine if it was someone she recognised or a stranger. She could usually tell whether it was someone she recognised as soon as they talked, but she struggled to identify individuals by their looks for the rest of her life. She had to rely on other clues such as their voices, the things they talked about, or a distinguishing feature such as red curly hair or dark brows to aid her.

Most of us assume that our brains analyse the complex features of faces and store extensive memories about them to identify a familiar face. We are unaware of how the brain shapes our world.

How can we escape a brain that continually makes our environment appear hazardous once we understand that we are spending our lives with a brain that processes and interprets our reality for us? How can we stop ideas of contamination from dominating our minds? How do we overcome the fear that we could hurt someone or that we have cancer growing in our bodies? How can we overcome our fear of driving a car if we experience it every time we try? The brain is no longer assisting us in comprehending and adapting to our surroundings. It's become a torture chamber!

How do you escape if your brain has become your torture chamber? If you have obsessive-compulsive disorder (OCD), you need an address to this issue even more. You need answers about how thc brain works so you can comprehend how to break free from the grip of OCD. The fact is that your brain functions according to a set of rules and constraints. We can use the laws and processes that regulate the brain's functioning to give us more control over our lives once we grasp how it operates. Knowing, for example, that the brain can only focus attention on one item at a time is a crucial tool of self-defence for someone suffering from obsessive thinking. You need to learn how to take advantage of this restriction in your brain, giving you a tool to acquire more control over the thoughts and anxieties that bother you. Once you grasp the functions of the OCD brain, as we'll call it, you'll be able to manage it more effectively.

Just as you need to learn enough about how your car works to keep it in excellent working order, you also need to understand enough about your brain to get it to work in a way that makes you more comfortable. Obsessions or persistent anxieties in your mind are analogous to an automobile with a specific flaw or malfunction. Knowing what's wrong with your car's engine might help you figure out how to fix it. You may need to keep an eye on the oil and add some frequently.

What Causes OCD?

It's natural to question what's wrong with your brain if you have OCD. Is there a bug or a malfunction? We all have flaws and faults in our brains; no one has a flawless brain. Each human being is distinct and one-of-a-kind, resulting from a remarkable complex process of cell union and division, merging genetics from two separate people. Unlike automobiles, which are tested, developed, and modified to reduce issues, this procedure is not intended to produce perfectly functioning brains. Every person's brain has different strengths and limitations. The most we can do is use our brains' capabilities, educate our brains to learn as effectively as we can, and avoid dealing with areas of life that demand the use of less competent brain functions. Some brains excel in mathematics, for example, and will make a person a brilliant accountant, but others should avoid that career. Some OCD sufferers have minds that will focus hard on minute aspects of a scenario for hours, dissatisfied until everything is perfect. That type of mind can make a person a cautious and precise writer, but it can also bring problems in other situations, such as never being on time because you don't feel ready to leave the house until everything is perfect. We may change our brains and behaviours via learning and skill development, but we all have strengths and limitations, many of which are connected to the brain we inherited.

The frontal lobes in the cortex, the basal ganglia, and connections between the frontal lobes and the amygdala (pronounced uh-MIG-dull-ah) are all linked to OCD. The question now is why do these brain structures behave differently in people with OCD. We observed that OCD and other anxiety disorders appear to run in families, implying that they are inherited somehow. You are more prone to experience anxiety if you have an anxious parent. Adoption studies have revealed that it is not only a matter of being raised by a worried parent; a hereditary component plays a role in these illnesses. However, genetics is not the only element to consider. We also learn about our unique anxieties and concerns via our personal experiences, families, and friends. In other words, your brain's OCD-related processes result from inherited inclinations and lived events.

Furthermore, experts have shown that viruses that affect the brain can cause obsessive thinking and other anxiety symptoms. PANDAS (Paediatric Autoimmune Neuropsychiatric Disorder Associated with Streptococcus) and PANS (Paediatric Autoimmune Neuropsychiatric Disorder Associated with Streptococcus) are two viruses that generally affect children aged three to twelve (Paediatric Acute-Onset Neuropsychiatric Syndrome). These viruses harm the basal ganglia, causing obsessive thinking, compulsive behaviour, and tics. When a kid develops OCD due to PANDAS or PANS, the symptoms are likely to appear shortly after the child contracts the virus, with no prior sign that OCD is an issue.

Brain structures are causing OCD symptoms, regardless of whether those structures are altered by heredity, disease, or learning experiences. What's most essential for you to understand is that OCD is not your fault, and you should not blame yourself for it. On the other hand, you must learn about what you're dealing with and how to deal with it since you deserve a better life than one hampered by OCD. OCD symptoms may be highly disruptive in your life, and knowing how your brain creates them can help you reduce their influence.

Obsessive Thinking In OCD

Obsessive thinking occurs when ideas appear to repeat in seemingly unending loops. Obsessive thinking manifests itself in a variety of ways. Worry is the most frequent type, and it refers to thoughts about what may go wrong and potential bad results. Worries frequently begin with "What if..." and conclude with terrifying notions of what may happen. Worries fluctuate from day to day, depending on the circumstances. People often and consciously engage in worry, yet some people find it difficult to manage. Worrying may become time-consuming and uncontrollable for those with OCD.

Obsessions are a subset of obsessive thinking. Obsessions, like anxieties, entail recurrent thought, but they are more constant than worries, which fluctuate from day to day. For example, even when he is receiving high marks, George always concentrates on the particular concept that he might not complete his college degree. Obsessions are unwelcome ideas that cannot be ignored. Obsessions might be concerns, but they can also be visions or impulses. For example, Deborah's mind keeps replaying the picture of her little brother getting hit by a car, and she can't get it out of her brain. When Gary is driving on the freeway, he frequently has the impulse to drive in front of a semi-truck, and he worries about what it means, even though he never acts on it. Obsessions can also be doubts about whether or not you did something or a constant focus on deciding what to do. You may be constantly concerned about whether you left your electric hair straightener on, or it may take you more than an hour to pick what type of tea to drink. Obsessions might be pictures of horrible perils that could befall you or others you care about. Sometimes they are strict orders that you believe you must obey because they are expectations for how you "should" do things. Some obsessive ideas involve highly unusual or impossible circumstances yet cannot be ignored, such as the possibility that you ran over a puppy on your way to work and didn't realise it.

Worries can arise from a variety of circumstances and subjects. Almost every scenario can be crafted into concern by the human brain. Just thinking about what may go wrong in such circumstances causes you to be concerned. Obsessions are more likely to fall into one of several groups or themes. Contamination is one topic, with concerns about being exposed to dirt, pathogens, viruses, and so on. Amy, for example, is afraid to eat anything at the market since she doesn't know where or how the food was produced. Another recurring motif is orderliness: things, activities, and even motions must be properly ordered or follow a predetermined order. Drawer contents, automobiles in the driveway, holiday dinners, and even hand motions while conversing might become a source of anxiety. Some people's obsessions might revolve around violence and hostility. A recruit on a college football team may have a persistent fear of hurting someone during his high school career, even though he has no recollection of doing so. People may have urges or visions of executing a violent or sexual act and fear that they will do so, even though the concept distresses them.

Perfectionism is a frequent motif of compulsive thinking in individuals suffering from OCD. Individuals with perfectionism are preoccupied with avoiding defects in their appearance or mistakes in their conduct, despite the reality that they cannot attain perfection as humans. One young girl could not stand her piano lessons because, when the instructor displayed an assigned musical piece, the girl could never hope to play it as well as the instructor did during her session. A graduate student in English was paralysed in her dissertation writing because no sentence in her first draft seemed to measure up to her idea of "dissertation level" writing.

Others concentrate on delicate issues such as religion or sexuality. A man may be concerned that he has no chance of entering heaven because God knows everything he thinks, and he may constantly bc looking for ways to atone for the angry thoughts he had about his parents as a child. Or a woman may be concerned that she is a lesbian despite having no attraction to women. We don't know why some people are obsessed with specific topics, but the same brain process underpins all obsessions—the only difference is the topic.

Obsessive thinking has the potential to take over a person's life. A college student may be concerned that his girlfriend does not love him and may contact her several times a day for reassurance. On her way to work, a mother may imagine her house on fire, worrying she left the stove on and turning back to check, making her late for work every day. A nanny may be concerned that she may take a knife from the wooden block on the counter and stab the children as they sleep, prompting her to resign. The same troubling ideas keep coming back. They often take up more than an hour every day, sometimes wholly dominating the individual's waking hours. Obsessive thoughts frequently motivate people to cope with them or neutralise them in some manner, which often leads to compulsions.

Compulsions are recurrent actions or mental activities that a person participates in to respond to a feared idea or circumstance or alleviate discomfort. They can take various forms, such as inspecting, counting, cleaning, and seeking reassurance. Compulsions, like obsessions, can start to rule your life because they provide a fast fix that allows you to ignore habits or anxieties and the stress they bring. When Damien becomes anxious when stuck in traffic on the highway, he mentally adds the numbers on the license plates of the automobiles in front of him. He realises it makes no sense and may be highly distracting, but he believes it protects him somehow. Perhaps you are anxious about the disorder of the medication bottles in the medical cabinet, but when you organise them, the worry subsides. When you carry out a compulsion, you feel less anxious about particular thoughts or circumstances, and the relaxation you feel rewards you for engaging in that activity. The compulsion grows greater as a result of the alleviation. So, what's the issue? The issue is that your comfort is just fleeting. You'll soon find yourself having to repeat the compulsion.

Obsessions And Worries In The Brain

The human brain evolved millions of years ago in an environment quite different from the one we live in today. Our brains' connections and functions evolved to enable humans to live in a world where they were hunters, gatherers, and prey. The connections and functions in our brain evolved to be utilised in new ways as people learned to farm and create communities, but the process of adaptation was not what you might anticipate. People sometimes talk about the brain adjusting to new demands and possibilities as if it were a rebuilt house, with new rooms and stairs being built and new appliances being added. That couldn't be farther from the truth. The connections and functions in the brain have mostly stayed unchanged throughout generations, much like an old log home that has had a wall removed but has the same furnishings and appliances from a century ago.

Some areas of our brain grew larger and more complexly organised throughout time, but when we compare our brains to those of early humans, as well as those of other animals, we discover many of the same pathways and processes. Although we have routes and processes that other animals do not have, particularly in our frontal lobes, all of the novel pathways are linked to pathways that have been running essentially unmodified since we lived as hunter-gatherers. A good comparison would be that the old cabin now has a lean-to constructed onto it to serve as a library, with many contemporary books on the shelves, but the cabin itself still has the old fireplace and all of the rough-hewn wooden furniture always had. Although the information is available in the library's volumes, no new kitchen or heating system has been constructed. Similarly, many areas of our brain have not been rebuilt to accommodate our contemporary lifestyles. We have some more circuitry in our cortex that gives new capacities, higher-level thinking, and improved capacity to store knowledge, but the core structure and functioning of the brain have not changed. This means that, while we can think in ways that other animals do not, these brain areas are linked to older sections of our brain that work as if we were still possible prey for hazardous creatures. We have an intricate defence mechanism woven into our brain and body's neural pathways that still influences our daily responses to threat in several ways. This protective mechanism contributes to the symptoms and discomfort associated with OCD, and rather than assisting us, our brain's more recently developed thinking abilities can create ideas and pictures that make the brain more likely to activate the defensive system.

Some of the thinking talents that have their roots in this freshly formed area of our brain include worry and compulsive thinking. The lobes of the brain behind our forehead, adequately known as the frontal lobes, became larger as humans evolved as a species, providing us with new abilities that other animals do not have. One of these abilities is anticipation, or the ability to consider what could happen before it does. This skill originated in a region of the brain that regulates our emotions, which makes sense. If the frontal lobes are responsible for movement in our arms and legs, then gaining the capacity to predict what could happen would assist us in making appropriate motions. It would be beneficial to have the capacity to anticipate before moving when hunting and reacting to physical dangers.

However, expectation in the human brain evolved beyond merely movement-related anticipation and into a complex mechanism that eventually included the human ability to envisage events and objects that one has never seen before. This ability, combined with the ability to plan (also rooted in the frontal lobes), resulting in all kinds of uniquely human behaviour, from learning to grow our food to building remarkable structures, ultimately resulting in scores of amazing activities imagined and eventually planned by humans, including space travel.

This incredible ability of the human brain to anticipate is a gift in many respects, but it comes with a cost. We can envision many disturbing occurrences, from breaking an essential object to imagining how we will kill someone - ideas that reflect events that may or may not occur. And these beliefs hurt the human race. We may fret and obsess over numerous thoughts and pictures, and while we do, we experience emotional reactions comparable to what we would feel if the incident truly happened. This is because the new regions of the human brain that generate these ideas and pictures are linked to the rest of the brain. Unfortunately, the remainder of the brain has not been altered so that it can respond differently to imagined risks than to genuine dangers. When you envisage an incident, your brain's defence systems frequently react as if it were happening, preparing you to react physically and causing changes in other regions of the brain and body that your conscious brain perceives in a profoundly emotional way. Understanding how various areas of the brain and body are linked might help you comprehend what is going on when you are plagued by concerns and obsessive thoughts or compelled to participate in recurrent compulsive activities. More significantly, this comprehension can show you how to break out from the vicious cycle that OCD can generate.

Pathways In The Brain That Create OCD

Obsessive thoughts and anxieties are generated in the brain's cortex, which is the vast, convoluted grey structure that occupies the upper section of your skull. The cortex's primary function is to interpret sensory information from our sense organs, such as our ears and eyes, so that we may understand what we hear and identify the significance of what we see. The cortex is important in determining if what we see, hear, smell, and so on is something to be concerned about. And the cortex not only assists us in recognising what is happening around us, but it also assists us in observing our own conduct and determining if we have made a mistake. The cortex is also where body reactions and motions are perceived and initiated. These cortical mechanisms are critical for responding to danger signals in our life. However, if the cortex detects danger, it is not the sole organ that responds. Other regions of the brain are also activated to mobilise a reaction to the danger.

The amygdala is a distinct region of your brain that begins the body's most efficient reaction to threats. Surprisingly, the amygdala can detect threats before the brain. This implies that, in some instances, the amygdala might cause your body to respond to protect you before you ever realise what you're seeing or hearing. You may even recall instances of this happening in your own life. One frequent example is driving on the highway and reacting to a threat so quickly that you take action (turn the wheel swiftly or press the brake) before you understand what you were reacting to.

Because there are two distinct pathways in the brain that receive information about possible dangers at different speeds, you can respond before realising what is occurring. Both routes begin when information from the senses travels through multiple channels to the thalamus, a walnut-shaped structure in the middle of your brain that chooses where to direct the information. One system, which we will call the amygdala pathway, analyses information about possible dangers very fast, travelling from sensory pathways to the thalamus and then directly to the amygdala. This permits the amygdala, which is located near the thalamus, to quickly receive sensory information. The second pathway begins similarly to the first, with sensory pathways delivering information to the thalamus, but it is referred to as the cortical pathway because the thalamus transmits sensory information up into the cortex to be processed. The information can then be accessed by the amygdala, which has numerous connections up into the cortex. The cortical route takes longer because sensory information must be transmitted from the thalamus to the cortex and then processed by multiple cortex regions before the amygdala can access it.

Why is it important to understand the two brain processes involved in sensing possible danger? Because these pathways play a significant role in the mechanisms that underpin OCD. We are fortunate in that much study has been conducted over the last many decades to investigate how the human brain identifies and responds to possible dangers. In laboratories all across the world, scientists have been studying the neural foundations of fear and anxiety. In both humans and animals, researchers have found brain regions that sense dangers and trigger defensive reactions. New imaging techniques, such as functional magnetic resonance imaging (fMRI) and positron emission tomography (PET), have provided us with pictures of how various human brain regions behave in a range of scenarios. This new information allows neuroscientists to piece together a comprehensive view of the mechanisms that lead to fear and anxiety in the human brain, offering an insight that transcends our comprehension of all other human emotions. Fear and anxiety are the precise sensations that you need to understand if you have OCD.

In brief, the brain generates thoughts and pictures, while the amygdala begins many of the emotional and physical elements of fear and concern that you encounter when coping with OCD. A rudimentary knowledge of the two anxiety pathways can help you understand how and why your brain creates and maintains painful, intrusive thoughts, as well as discover techniques to break free from the never-ending cycle of OCD that is restricting your life.

The Self-Defeating Cycle Of OCD

Because of the cortical route, ideas in the cortex can stimulate the amygdala, resulting in the stress and anxiety feelings we experience. It may help envision the amygdala "watching" what is going on in the cortex, similar to how a toddler may watch television. The amygdala responds to scary pictures or ideas created in the cortex by producing a defensive reaction in the body, which we feel like fear and anxiety, just as a kid may react to a scary movie with fear. This, in turn, raises the level of anxiety about the feelings. Essentially, the terrible ideas cause a frightening physiological reaction, which causes anxiety and intensifies the attention on the frightening thoughts. You can see how this process may become a vicious circle in which thoughts cause worry, anxiety causes greater concern about and attention to your thoughts, and anxiety causes even more anxiety.

It's tough to divert your attention away from something that appears to be dangerous. In reality, it is the amygdala's responsibility to keep you aware of possible danger. Thus it becomes engaged in keeping you focused on these intrusive ideas. You're no longer only dealing with intrusive thoughts; you're also coping with anxiousness. You start focusing on methods to reduce anxiety rather than ways to reduce intrusive thoughts. Once you grasp the roles of the amygdala and cortex in this cyclical process, you'll be able to apply your understanding of the two routes to solve the problem.

In essence, OCD is a self-defeating cycle that begins with unpleasant thoughts and then produces worry, which causes the thoughts to become even more uncomfortable and turns the problem into a struggle against anxiety. You may develop compulsions to assist in alleviating your worry, leading to full-blown OCD.

Can I Change My Brain?

Scientists have discovered that the brain has an incredible ability to remodel its architecture and rearrange its response patterns in only the previous three decades. This is referred to as neuroplasticity. Your brain is not fixed and unchanging, as many people, including scientists, previously thought. The circuits in your brain are created not only by heredity but also by your experiences and how you think and behave. You can change your brain's response no matter how old you are. Of course, there are limits, but your brain has a surprising amount of flexibility and capacity for development. This involves altering a brain that has a penchant for intrusive, unpleasant thoughts that lead to compulsions.

New connections in the brain frequently form in very basic ways that you may not have considered: Aerobic exercise has been proven to cause changes in the architecture and physiology of the brain, which are followed by quantifiable mood changes. Certain medicines aid in the development and modification of brain circuits. Psychotherapy has also been found to induce changes, such as decreasing activity in one part of the brain while boosting activation in others. People who have been taught mindfulness meditation, in particular, exhibit alterations in the connections between regions of the brain that regulate anxiety. We'll discuss how these strategies can aid you in your struggle against OCD in the coming chapters, but for now, know that you can reprogram your brain!

We know a lot about modifying the brain to minimise upsetting thoughts, produce them less frequently, and respond to them differently. As we go through this book, we will show you how to stop the OCD brain's response patterns and educate the OCD brain to respond according to new patterns by constructing new neural structures that enable more anxiety-resistant responses. This is what we mean when we say you're "rewiring" your OCD brain. Of course, there is no true "wire" in the brain, but interestingly, distinct neurological structures in our brain do utilise electrical impulses to interact, and they send messages to each other via connections that function similarly to wiring. Understanding how the various regions of the brain communicate will give you far more power over this communication, allowing you to exercise more control over these processes than you could previously. Furthermore, if you understand how certain areas of the brain learn and create new connections, you will be able to rewire or train the various sections of your brain to behave in new ways.

The techniques described in this book will assist you in using the neuroplasticity of the brain and understanding the two pathways that cause anxiety to make long-term changes in your brain that will offer you greater control over your life. My objective is to assist you in handling toxic thoughts in time and modifying the way your brain typically responds to these thoughts so that they become less bothersome in your life. You may also utilise the knowledge in this book to change the structure of your brain so that it fights worry rather than creating it. My goal is to provide you with the information you need to escape the torture dungeon that your OCD brain may create.

3

The Myths Surrounding Toxic Thoughts

There are several common misconceptions regarding toxic thoughts that lead to intrusive ideas getting entrenched. Dispelling these beliefs with facts will go a long way toward changing your attitude about your mind.

We all have ideas about what our thoughts say about us. Many of us feel that what goes through our heads reveals something about the person we are inside. Some of our notions about our thoughts may be true, but we now know that many prevalent views are wrong, and these mistaken beliefs can lead to a lot of misery.

Every day, experts discover more about thinking and your ideas about the type of person you are. Some long-held beliefs about what thoughts signify and what sorts of thoughts have been challenged by recent research. This chapter debunks common misconceptions regarding thoughts that contribute to unwelcome intrusive thoughts. Because each myth adds to the tendency to become fixated on undesirable intrusive thoughts, it makes sense to analyse each one and determine how much weight you place on each myth. Each one is demonstrably untrue, according to psychological studies.

Our Thoughts Are Under Our Control

Many individuals mistakenly assume that because our ideas are under our conscious control, we should regulate them.

Fact: Many of our thoughts and ideas are not conscious ones. This is a reality that we appreciate at times. An insight or inspiration can aid in the resolution of an issue. If you ask a poet or singer how she comes up with lyrics, she could answer it just "comes to her". Sometimes an idea may suddenly spring into your head, like a mental tic or hiccup. Inquire with anybody who practices meditation. We don't have control over it, and we're not liable for it. Thoughts come and go. They wander. They are fluttering about. They do not take orders.

It occasionally smacks you in the face when you have no control over your thoughts. When listening to dull speeches, everyone's mind wanders. A loud environment might disrupt your train of thought. And when was the last time you considered an argument at home while conversing with someone at work? How often do you tell yourself to be confident, only to see self-criticism and doubts coming in?

Just because you can imagine certain ideas on purpose does not imply you have control over them. You can't just make your thoughts go away. You can direct your attention to certain thoughts, but it doesn't imply you can make them disappear.

Worried Voice: I wish I had more control over my thoughts, especially when they are bad. I'm afraid I'm ill.

False Comfort: What you really need is some mental fortitude. Make an extra effort!

. . .

Concerned Voice: I'm trying, but I can't seem to pull it off. I think I'm in chaos.

Wise Mind: Everyone's mind wanders. It may be fascinating to see. I don't need to put a halt to any of it. Neither do you. Thoughts are just thoughts that occur.

Worried Voice and **False Comfort** both believe in the illusion that controlling one's thoughts, particularly troubling ones, is feasible and crucial for mental wellness. They are entirely incorrect. A **Wise Mind** understands better.

Belief in the idea that you control your thoughts leads to the widespread but useless notion that you may replace unpleasant thoughts with good ones and control what you think. The facts indicate that you may actively think good ideas and shift your attention briefly from undesirable thoughts to preferred ones. However, the ideas you attempt to replace tend to endure and frequently return to your attention even more forcibly. How many times have you attempted to dismiss an idea just to have it resurface?

Our Thoughts Indicate Our Character

Another thought myth is that thoughts disclose our character or underlying intents and that certain individuals have a dark side that is only apparent in their thoughts.

Fact: We all know that ideas have little to do with personality. Character is a thought of how you lead your life. It has to do with what you choose to do or do not do. Thoughts are the things that go through your head. When thoughts just happen, it is not your decision. When there is no opportunity for choice, there is no room for character issues. A thought is not a fact or a personal opinion. Character is defined by the decisions you make in life, not by what comes to mind.

In popular culture, complex metaphors are frequently used to explain this misconception. The terrifying instances are of seemingly flawless lovely people being taken over by their evil side, whether through the metaphor of werewolves, possession, Jekyll and Hyde, or some other means of innocent people turning into killers. Movies like The Exorcist, American Psycho, and Forbidden Planet are intended to frighten viewers into believing that, no matter how pure or well-intentioned you are, there is an evil power within you waiting to take control. These delusions feed the erroneous belief that one's underlying ideas disclose true intents or nature even when denied as if there is an inner monster that may jump out against your will.

Similarly, movies and books portraying society's disintegration, such as Lord of the Flies, Mad Max, and other post-apocalyptic horrors, imply that our survival impulses may transform us into moral monsters. They all indicate that we are on the verge of becoming civilised. Taking it a step further suggests that uncivilised ideas are only the tip of the iceberg and that one's actual nature or character may not be what it appears to be.

Surprisingly, people frequently apply this misconception exclusively to themselves and their own thinking. If a buddy expresses a bizarre, repulsive, or illogical notion, you are quick to reassure him that minds are fickle, that these thoughts are meaningless, and that you still respect him. It's simple to make fun of someone else's disturbing thoughts.

Concerned Voice: I always have filthy ideas, even about children. Deep down, I must be a horrible guy. It occurs regularly.

False Comfort: Don't be ridiculous. We both know you're great. Fill in the gaps with perverted thoughts. Thinking about it may cause you to doubt yourself.

. . .

Voice of Concern: I try, but it just keeps occurring. I'm wondering whether anything horrible happened to me that I'm not aware of and is now set in my subconscious. People who have been mistreated are said to become abusers.

False Hope: People may overcome their negative thoughts. All you have to do is be optimistic.

Worried Voice and **False Comfort** both think that ideas reflect the character and struggle to deal with this in this discussion. They are both succumbing to this illusion.

Our Thoughts Indicate The Inner Self

This notion is that thoughts are pathways to our inner selves, similar to how eyes are windows to the soul. This includes the notion that whatever is in our minds represents our actual thoughts and feelings, regardless of how much we protest. So pervasive ideas must reveal some particular, maybe hidden, reality about ourselves.

Everyone has strange, aggressive, or insane ideas from time to time. If every thought spoke to an underlying character, 90% of individuals would be strange, aggressive, or insane. About 90% of people admit to having intrusive ideas that they describe as strange, aggressive, frightening, or insane. Consider some of the popular horror films and television series these days. Perhaps you are unable to view them because they make you feel too scared. But keep in mind that regular, creative individuals create these horrible, strange, aggressive, and insane circumstances. They are just writing scripts that others will see.

This myth implies that strange or illogical ideas may signify a loss of control over your mind or possibly mental disease. Another erroneous inference is that having intrusive, unpleasant thoughts means you are a deviant or disgusting person.

People who have unwelcome aggressive or violent ideas may become afraid that they are violent or furious while not knowing these emotions and that these thoughts represent their real feelings. They may grow to believe not only that they must be horrible people at heart but that they must also exert significant control over these thoughts.

We all have mental activity outside of our consciousness, and it's fascinating to speculate on how particular mental processes occur. However, there is no validity to the notion that blips of intrusive thoughts and pictures disclose underlying truths and that thoughts reveal fundamentally important motivations, sentiments, and intentions or carry signals that must be addressed when they differ from conscious thoughts, feelings and intentions.

The Unconscious Mind Can Affect Actions

The notion is that our unconscious mind is a powerful force that guides our thoughts and activities, often in the dark and against our conscious minds and will. So there's a chance that unconscious energies will spring up against our will and drive us to act rashly, angrily, violently, or unjustly if we don't want to.

Fact: Analysing the meaning of Freudian slips and automatic connections, as well as the content of dreams, are common methods for attempting to comprehend the intricate workings of the unconscious mind. However, the fleeting idea of dropping your infant reveals no unconscious desire to cause damage. And having the sudden idea that you might leap over the balcony since the railing is low does not show any hidden unconscious suicidal desires.

Concerned Voice: Every day I take the train to work, I fantasise about pushing someone under the train. What does the idea that I have such negative thoughts say about me? Perhaps my subconscious mind will force me to do it.

False Comfort: Tell yourself you'd never do something violent. Don't allow those ideas to get the best of you. Distract yourself by focusing on anything else. Please pray for relief.

Worried Voice: I try, but the ideas persist.

False Comfort tries hard to comfort **Worried Voice** and gives coping methods to deal with the troubling ideas. While coping techniques may give momentary comfort, they do not last. Unfortunately, they both accept the illusion that such ideas are important parts of the unconscious mind that necessitate a reaction.

Another myth is the belief that doubtful thoughts are messages, signs, or cautions from the wiser and more sensitive unconscious. Some of you may have concerns about a decision and feel that this implies you made a mistake and that there is an important problem you need to address. According to this belief, a questioning thought is a communication from your unconscious that repeats itself to warn you to reconsider what you did or intend to do.

However, it is not true that frightening thoughts are fuelled by underlying wants or warnings to be taken seriously. There's an ancient adage that goes something like, "The want is father to the dread," which implies that your fear of doing something horrible is generated by your desire to do it. This is a myth with no evidence to back it up. It just serves one purpose: it adds to people's anxieties by causing unwelcome intrusive thoughts.

Thinking Something Makes It Likely To Happen

The foundation of this myth is the concept that believing something makes it more likely to happen or more true. Many individuals dislike the concept of having bad thoughts because they feel that having negative ideas would lead to more terrible events. Some think that the negative attracts the bad and the good attracts the positive.

Fact: This is an utter misinterpretation of what is known about thinking. Psychologists refer to this myth as thought-action fusion or magical thinking. The truth is that a thought does not provide a message about what will occur. Similarly, a thought is not a forewarning or forecast of a terrible deed or occurrence in the future. Thoughts do not forewarn aircraft crashes, car accidents, or natural calamities. Premonition is a feeling that occurs as a result of a thought; it is not an exact prediction of the future. We tend to recall the few premonitions that come true and forget the many other doubts and sensations that pass without being fulfilled.

Even more significantly, your ideas cannot cause unfavourable acts or situations to occur. In the actual world, thoughts do not affect probability. Thoughts cannot move objects or harm humans. Furthermore, ideas are not elements of your unconscious that may become uncaged and take control if you are not alert. Thinking that someone could die does not make him more likely to die; a passing idea about what it might be like to be unfaithful to a spouse does not drive you to seek an affair, and a quick terrified thought does not increase the likelihood of genuine danger or tragedy. Please don't mix up thoughts with facts. A fact can either be true or untrue. A thought is nothing more than a thought. Thoughts are frequently our educated assumptions about the world around us and how it appears to function. Thoughts do not influence the physical world.

But, you may be wondering, 'if I have bad ideas, won't I do more terrible things?'

To some extent, it is correct. Your attitude and motivation might shift as a result of your thoughts and beliefs. Here's an illustration:

If you feel that something will be terrifying, you will approach it with caution, and you may even opt to avoid it because you are unsure that you will be able to handle the fear. And if you fear your boss would be upset if you leave early on Tuesday to attend your son's soccer final, you could decide to call in sick or skip the game. In other words, our beliefs and ideas might occasionally impact what we do. However, this is not the same as the myth that thinking about something increases the likelihood of it happening.

Thinking Something Makes It Unlikely To Happen

This myth is nearly the polar opposite of the previous one. It is specifically that contemplating something will make it less likely to happen or less true. You may feel that worrying about someone you care about is a means of safeguarding that person, demonstrating love and commitment, and preventing terrible things from happening. Staying immersed with concerned thoughts appears to be a method of keeping attentive — and so more prepared — for danger.

Fact: Once again, in the actual world, thoughts do not affect probability. While worrying about someone may make you feel as if you are doing something to protect him or her you are just training your brain to promote a continuous cycle of worry. Keep in mind that emotions are not facts. Feeling the urge to keep involved by continually thinking about someone is succumbing to anxiety's false alarms.

Only Sick People Have Intrusive Thoughts

This relates to the erroneous notion that only those who are disturbed experience intrusive or strange thoughts.

. . .

Fact: No one is completely free of strange, unpleasant, and distressing fleeting ideas. This implies that almost everyone you know, including your friends, work colleagues, teachers, and physicians, has had intrusive thoughts. Mother Teresa, in reality, suffered unwanted intrusive thoughts (Teresa 2009). So, most likely, does your favourite celebrity, as well as your preacher.

The key distinction is that almost everyone has fleeting intrusive thoughts. Because they are repeated and occasionally stay entrenched, your intrusive thoughts seem extremely different. This gives them an especially unsettling feeling as if they are the result of a deranged mind. However, the persistence of these ideas has nothing to do with your character or your worth as a human being. And it has nothing to do with being a troubled individual. The stickiness is heavily influenced by how you think and feel about these ideas and the techniques and intensity with which you try to rid yourself of them.

Every Thought Is Worth Thinking

The meaning is that every idea is worth considering; it makes sense and is useful to investigate the substance of each thought that crosses your mind or comes to your notice.

Fact: You, like cable television, have several separate channels of thought running through your head at the same time. It is difficult to consider them all, and some of your channels are just full of garbage (like maybe the infomercial channel or the local high school announcements). Not all are worth contemplating. Assume you're listening to the radio and something went wrong, so instead of listening to one station at a time, you're listening to two, three, five, or ten at the same time. One channel may be wonderful music you want to listen to, while another could be an interesting debate. Others may be a dull repeat broadcast, the music you despise, or a tale you've heard a hundred times before. Without giving it any consideration, you would attempt to focus on the items that piqued your attention while ignoring the other channels.

Similarly, you have several "thought channels" running through your head. You can pick and select what to focus on most of the time without putting in a lot of work. Some ideas just appear to be more intriguing to explore than others. However, suppose you believe that all ideas are worth thinking about (i.e., there are no garbage channels of the mind). In that case, you may choose to focus on that one thought and give it significance and attention it does not deserve when an intrusive thought arises. Junk may take over your focus. This is especially true if you feel the intrusive idea is crucial or believe you have received a message, signal, or warning sign. In situations like these, you may become trapped, and the idea will keep battling through your mind, demanding your attention.

In reality, everyone's head is filled with garbage thoughts that aren't worth considering seriously. If we let our minds stray into meaningless thoughts, they will just pass us by.

Worried Voice: I'm trying to study, but all I can think about is whether or not I should marry my boyfriend.

False Comfort: You've just been dating for a few weeks. Don't even think about it right now. You must study.

Worried Voice: I know, but I feel like I should think about it because I'm afraid he'll ask me.

False Comfort: Do you believe that means he will ask you?

Concerned Voice: Sort of. Isn't it true that I should be prepared? What if he does approach me? I really should be studying. If I fail the exam tomorrow, I may lose my scholarship.

False Comfort: Remember what you went through with the previous guy?

. . .

Worried Voice: But this time, it feels like there's a serious problem.

Wise Thought: Hey, you're both enjoying the nonsense channel. It does not necessitate your attention simply because it occurred to you. Simply because someone throws a football at you does not obligate you to catch it. All the time, trash channels throw junk at us.

Thoughts That Repeat Are Important

You may assume that thoughts that repeat themselves must be significant. After all, it appears that if an idea is unimportant, it will simply fly out of our minds and be forgotten. The fact that the notion continues coming back must indicate that it is meaningful.

Fact: The significance of a notion has very little to do with how many times it is repeated. If an idea is fought or pushed aside, it tends to repeat itself. So, if you have a recurring idea that you are resisting, it will begin to fade away when you stop opposing it. Any idea you try to suppress is more likely to resurface, such as 'Don't worry about that itch', 'Stop replaying that commercial jingle in your head,' or Stop noticing the bit of food between her teeth.'

This is how your brain truly works. Spending energy on a thought strengthens brain connections and increases the likelihood that the idea will occur. This works with any notion; it has nothing to do with its significance. The simple reality is that your efforts to block certain thoughts from entering your head are what causes them to resurface and feel trapped. What occurs when you try to quit thinking while falling asleep is one example of this. Everyone has witnessed ideas expand, elaborate, and recur the more we try to reject them and "stop thinking." To fall asleep naturally, we must be prepared to let our minds roam and not fight them.

I hope you now better grasp some of the most frequent misunderstandings and misconceptions regarding how ideas function in people's heads. As a result, you are better equipped to comprehend the undesirable intrusive ideas presently bothering you, how they became entrenched, and how to interact with them in a new way. They don't mean what you believe they mean; there's no need to be afraid of them, and rejecting them won't make them disappear.

Believing even any of these misconceptions might cause regular intrusive thoughts to become entrenched. Knowing the truth about these popular beliefs will make intrusive thoughts less likely to remain around. Now that we've debunked the myths, we'll address some of the frequently asked questions in the next chapter.

4

What's Been Holding You Back?

We've seen how anxiety in the brain may exacerbate the obsessive process and lead to a self-defeating loop. The amygdala, the brain's root of anxiety, is examined in this chapter. Remembering that the brain is a physical organ regulated by physical processes will help you cope with your OCD symptoms. Recognising that your anxiety is founded on a physiological mechanism to protect you from threats will help you. The mechanisms that give birth to our feelings of fear and anxiety begin when the amygdala becomes engaged and creates a defence reaction to anything seen as a danger. Understanding that the defensive mechanism begun in the amygdala causes your anxiety is critical to eliminating the symptoms of anxiety in OCD. Reducing anxiety by concentrating on its origins in the amygdala is more successful than compulsions in the long run, and knowing the amygdala's response will also help you behave differently to your anxiety and obsessions.

Your amygdala, not your cognitive processes, is responsible for the physical responses in your body and brain that cause worry. If you have a racing heart or feel nauseous, unsteady, or dizzy, you can thank your amygdala. Suppose you understand how and why the amygdala produces these bodily reactions. In that case, you'll be able to accomplish two important goals: you'll interpret the meaning of your anxiety more properly, and you'll have greater control over your anxiety experience. The objective is to minimise the frequency of your worry as well as your discomfort about it. This will give you an advantage when it comes to obsessions and compulsions.

The amygdala (the Greek word for almond, which also reflects its shape) is the origin of the fight-or-flight response. We really have two amygdalae, both in the centre of the brain, but it has been customary to refer to the amygdala in the single, and we shall do so here. We shall not discuss the distinctions between the two amygdalae because they are not necessary for our goals.

The amygdala's position in the middle of the brain places it near some of the brain's most significant regions, including the hypothalamus, giving it the capacity to make fast adjustments in the functioning of your heart, lungs, muscles, and even digestive system. When your amygdala detects a threat of any type, it is programmed to initiate a complicated response in your body that will allow you to protect yourself. Because it occurs before the brain has finished processing the sensory information that the amygdala is responding to, the amygdala can produce this protective reaction before you are even aware of a risk. Knowing the source and purpose of this defence reaction will help you better understand what you're going through as you strive to manage your stress and anxiety.

The Amygdala As An Early Warning Alarm System

Natural selection has shaped the human amygdala into a danger detector whose primary aim is to keep you safe. (It should be noted that the amygdala also plays other roles, such as positive emotional reactions and aggressiveness, but that is not the book's subject.) As you go about your day, your amygdala is on the lookout for anything that might suggest a possible threat and is ready to launch a defence reaction to keep you safe. Because of the way the brain is constructed, the amygdala can function as an early warning system and defensive coordinator, which has kept our ancestors safe for generations.

This section will look closely at the amygdala's involvement in the two routes mentioned earlier. You may recall that sensory information enters the thalamus and is transmitted straight to the amygdala through the amygdala route. The thalamus transmits incoming sensory information is transmitted to the cortex by the thalamus before reaching the amygdala through the cortical route. Because these two brain pathways each result in the sensation of anxiety, which drives both obsessions and compulsions, it is critical to track both routes.

Cortical Route: When you receive information through your eyes, ears, or other sense organs, it must be processed in the cortex pathway before you can perceive it. Information goes from the sensory organs to the thalamus at the centre of the brain.

The thalamus functions similarly to an office receptionist, receiving information from the many sense organs and sending it to the cortex for processing. For example, the visual information from your eyes while you read this book is delivered first to the thalamus, and then the thalamus sends it on to be processed at the back of your brain in the occipital lobes of your cortex. In contrast, sensory information from your fingers when you pet a cat in your lap travels up your spinal cord into your thalamus, which then sends it up to the parietal lobes, a part of your cortex where touch information is processed. Only when the occipital or parietal lobes digest the information can you see the words you're reading or feel the silky hair of the cat. Fortunately, this information exchange takes only a fraction of a second.

Amygdala Pathway: The thalamus, the neural receptionist, has a little safety net as well. At the same time that the thalamus delivers sensory information to the appropriate place in the brain for processing, it also sends the information straight to your amygdala. The amygdala is adjacent to the thalamus; as a result, the amygdala receives information faster than the other regions of your brain. The amygdala is an excellent early warning system, processing information fast to determine its significance. Because you rely on the comparatively slower processing of the separate lobes in your brain to absorb information, your amygdala can see, hear, and feel things before you can.

Information flows from your sense organs (eyes, ears, skin) to your thalamus, then to your cortex, and ultimately to your amygdala through the cortical route. This is the slower of the two paths, although it still takes less than a second. Everything you feel originates from this channel because what you see, hear, and feel is dependent on the cortex. Within milliseconds, the information goes from your sense organs to your thalamus and then directly to your amygdala through the amygdala route, resulting in anxiety. The amygdala continually monitors what you are feeling at a faster rate than you can. You can't see or hear the amygdala's sensory information since you rely on the cortex for information. You don't know why your muscles are stiff, or your pulse is beating, but you are aware of the physiological responses or defensive responses that the amygdala creates when it perceives a possible threat.

Let's take a look at one of the most typical scenarios in which you could have encountered these routes in action. Assume you're travelling along the highway when another automobile unexpectedly merges into your lane. You've yanked the wheel to the left and drove your car into the grass on the side of the highway before you can think. You slam the brakes and come to a complete halt, reviewing what has just occurred in your head. You nearly feel as if someone else yanked the wheel to the left because you have no memory of thinking about what to do; you just did it. Fortunately, you did the right thing and avoided a collision. Alternatively, we might argue that your amygdala escaped the collision. Take a look at the two paths we mentioned before. When the automobile swerved into your lane, the information from your eyes was sent to the thalamus, which then routed it to the occipital lobe at the rear of your brain. However, processing this information took some time. Simultaneously, the amygdala got information about the oncoming automobile from the thalamus and processed it more quickly. Your amygdala sensed the threat a fraction of a second before your brain (or you) did. Your amygdala was able to initiate the reflex of yanking the wheel to the left before you ever saw the automobile swerve into your lane. Your amygdala's quick reaction might have saved your life!

It's worth noting that your amygdala's reaction was triggered by more than just your quick shift of the steering wheel. You undoubtedly felt a surge of adrenaline and a rapid spike in your heart rate as you made the swift movement to avoid the danger. People sometimes think that such a reaction is just a reflex, but it was not a reflex based on impulses from your spinal cord. When you burn your fingers, a reflex is triggered, and the pain signal travels to your spinal cord, which sends back a signal to withdraw your hand away from the heat. Reflexes occur before the message reaches your brain. Because the visual information in your brain had to be processed by your amygdala for you to jerk the steering wheel in this situation, it was not a reflex. Because your amygdala saw an incoming vehicle, you were able to respond quickly in defence. You acted before your cortex had a chance to recognise the issue and determine what to do.

Considering The Costs

You can see how the amygdala's capacity to perceive or hear possible hazards faster than the brain might be beneficial. Because of the way our brains are designed to deliver speedy information to the amygdala, our ancestors were able to respond quickly, saving them from many perils. However, receiving knowledge fast comes at a cost. The amygdala relies on raw, unprocessed sensory input via this direct channel rather than the comprehensive information obtained when the cortex analyses the information. Your cortex can analyse and understand circumstances more completely than the amygdala, allowing it to identify critical information that the amygdala may miss. So your amygdala is reacting to a hazy memory of what was heard or seen and acting quickly based on that shaky information. Consider what the amygdala perceives as a partly developed, hazy Polaroid photograph—it has four legs... Is it, then, a cow or a dog? Fortunately, incomplete knowledge is frequently sufficient to determine whether or not there is a risk. When speed isn't a problem, the amygdala can acquire more precise information from the brain as soon as the cortex analyses it.

A famous example of the relative accuracy of these two distinct paths was presented by Joseph LeDoux (1996). He hypothesised that if you are travelling through the woods and suddenly notice a brown, snake-like, curved thing on the route ahead of you, the amygdala may activate a defensive response, causing you to leap back with your pulse racing very quickly. However, based on the processing in your brain, you quickly identify that the brown item is a piece of vine rather than a snake. Even though your heart is still pounding, you feel a rush of relief. What happened?

The amygdala recognised a possible threat—the raw information from the thalamus suggested the item resembled a snake—and took care of developing a suitable defence reaction, which wasn't the case in this situation. You unnecessarily leapt back, and you most likely felt an adrenaline surge and increased muscular tension as a result. When the cortex processed the information a fraction of a second later, you detected features that the cortex could give and saw the item as non-threatening. The brain ultimately relayed information to the amygdala, allowing the amygdala to stop raising the alert. In terms of safety, we are better off as a species if our brains quickly defend us from possible threats—and then decide whether or not it was required. The amygdala's motto is "better safe than sorry."

An important lesson should not be neglected here: the amygdala's reaction to what you perceive may be incorrect and unnecessary. As you understand more about the amygdala, you discover that it does not make meticulous, knowledge-based, rational judgments but rather reacts based on partial information, with a predisposition toward reacting even when unneeded. Nonetheless, because the amygdala can trigger a wide range of physiological reactions based on its interpretation, many people misunderstand those bodily signals as indicating a genuine threat. When you experience anxiety due to the amygdala activating the defensive response, it's natural to think that there's a solid cause for your fear. This happened one day as Helen was carefully selecting her seat in a theatre. She sat down after deciding on a certain seat and noticed what appeared to be a spider on the arm of her seat. In a fraction of a second, she understood that the form was merely a knot in the wood that resembled a spider. (Her amygdala had erroneously responded, but her cortex could offer more comprehensive and accurate information.)

Nonetheless, Helen couldn't escape the sense that she shouldn't be sitting in this chair since her amygdala had triggered the defensive reaction, and her heart was pounding. Based on how she was feeling, she decided to purchase a new chair to ensure her safety. In other words, she was acting based on the amygdala's incorrect response.

Overestimation of dangers is particularly prevalent in OCD. The amygdala is involved in this issue. People frequently overestimate risks because they believe the amygdala's reaction is accurate. You can learn not always to believe your anxious experience once you know the amygdala's inclination to react incorrectly. Your fear is certainly genuine, yet it is frequently the result of an unneeded, erroneous defence reaction from the amygdala.

In short, human brains contain a built-in protective mechanism that hasn't changed much over millions of years and is quite comparable to the neuronal system in other species' brains. When activated, the amygdala produces genuine and profound changes in our bodies, resulting in a defence reaction. When the amygdala causes these physiological changes, we commonly experience dread and anxiety as emotional reactions. However, these emotional responses should not be relied on to identify danger constantly. Because the amygdala does not always have a correct perception of the circumstance, just feeling fear or anxiety does not validate the existence of a risk.

Defensive Options: The Fight, Flight, Or Freeze Response

Let's take a closer look at the amygdala's ability to generate a quick protective reaction. This response is commonly referred to as the fight-or-flight response, but research suggests it should be referred to as the fight, flight, or freeze (FFF) response. That's because when the amygdala perceives a possible threat, it quickly sends messages to various regions of the brain to help us respond, and the responses the amygdala may choose from are roughly classified into three categories: fight, flight, or freeze. We can **fight**, whether by hitting, shoving, or battling with someone or something. We can also leave the circumstance by engaging in **fleeing**, ducking to avoid an item, or avoiding situations. Finally, there is the option of **freezing** or being motionless or immovable. You may experience each of these sorts of reactions to hazardous events at different points in your life. You may also observe that one or two approaches are more likely for you, noting that you prefer to flee and avoid rather than fight, or vice versa. The idea is that these basic reactions are hardwired into us as preprogrammed defence mechanisms that the amygdala can swiftly trigger and adjust to the environment.

Consider that the amygdala's objective when it recognises a possible threat is to prepare us to fight, run, or freeze. To achieve this, it must activate a slew of physiological reactions. When the body has to move rapidly or with great power, the amygdala can quickly produce the required modifications in the body to allow these movements to take place. Fighting or escaping frequently necessitates a rise in blood pressure and blood supply from the heart. Because increased muscular tension and responsiveness are required, glucose is released into the circulation to fuel muscle reactions. At the same time, digestion is hindered because blood is redirected to muscles in the extremities, creating a nauseous feeling in your stomach. These processes must occur for the body to be prepared to respond to a threat, and the amygdala may activate all of them. Understanding the purpose of these physiological reactions might help you comprehend them when you have them. "My heart is racing because the amygdala is preparing me to fight." "My legs are trembling because my amygdala is tensing up my muscles to prepare me to flee." The fact is that these emotions frequently do not assist us in coping with the difficulties that we face.

Consider Brenda, preoccupied with performing her job right, including showing up on time, keeping her coworkers happy with her performance, and not bringing unwanted attention to herself. Brenda felt nauseated several mornings as she prepared to go to work and saw nausea as an indication that something was wrong.

The nausea was caused by a slowdown of digestive processes when the amygdala increased the FFF response to her work-related concerns. Despite the absence of a physical threat, Brenda's amygdala developed a defensive reaction to the threat of going to the office. Brenda fought through nausea and made it to work on time after realising that it was due to her FFF reaction and not because she was unwell or a major threat at work. She understood that focusing on and fretting about that sick feeling in her stomach was pointless. She wasn't sick; she just had the FFF reaction.

Brenda's queasiness subsided as she got to work and got busy performing her job. The amygdala was attempting to prepare her for a threat, but the FFF reaction was terminated when nothing alarming happened. Until Brenda realised what was going on, the amygdala's protective reaction was hindering her more than it was helping. If you reframe your anxiety experience and recognise it for what it is—a part of the amygdala's defensive response—anxiety will be less likely to feed your obsessions or compulsions. When you feel anxious, you typically think that there is a threat around. Actually, it usually implies that the amygdala is triggering the defence response.

Finally, when the amygdala generates the FFF response, it might have another significant influence. When the amygdala is engaged, it can seize control and overrule the cortex. The cortex does not function properly while the amygdala is creating a strong defensive reaction. Many neuronal connections connect the amygdala to the cortex, allowing the amygdala to substantially affect the cortex's response on a variety of levels, including directing attention to what the amygdala thinks essential. The amygdala may impact what we focus on, how accurately we process incoming information, what memories come to mind, and what actions we take because of its ability to override other brain processes. When people have difficulty concentrating or get paralysed in terror, they may believe they are losing control or going insane. This is referred to as an "amygdala hijack," The amygdala takes over, and the cortex is sidelined.

When your cortex is having difficulties focusing, it makes no sense to you, and you may think about what you are experiencing in your cortex in ways that increase your worry. Because Sophia can't focus on hearing the CEO's questions, she becomes concerned about more than just her job interview; she becomes concerned that she is losing control of her mind. People with OCD frequently fixate on these sorts of events and stress about the possibility that they will "go insane." However, it is entirely natural to be unable to focus your attention or order your thoughts when the amygdala has taken over your cortex. This does not imply that you are insane. When the amygdala perceives danger, the brain is essentially programmed to enable it to take charge. Instead of worrying about these events, you must learn how to control the cortex and its impact on the amygdala.

From The FFF Response To Feelings Of Fear And Anxiety

When the amygdala creates the FFF response, we experience numerous changes in our bodies, and while our brains analyse this defence response, we may experience a painful emotion: fear, anxiety, or dread. Let's look more closely at how the FFF response causes these emotional reactions. The amygdala does not directly create these feelings; instead, we require the brain to interpret our experiences in a way that allows us to be conscious of our emotional reactions. In the same way that the cortex assists us in processing information from our sense organs, it also provides us with awareness of our feelings. However, these sensations are founded on and controlled by the amygdala's protective response. This is why it's common to hear that the amygdala is the source of dread and anxiety, even if it's a little more nuanced than that.

To experience emotions, we must be aware of what is going on in our bodies and minds. Let's use a basic example—seeing—to explain how the brain works and why I don't want to suggest the amygdala causes dread and anxiety. You may be tempted to assert that you see with your eyes, yet your eyes do nothing more than receive light waves and convert them into electrical impulses that your brain can analyse. For you to perceive anything, certain regions of your brain must receive and analyse electrical impulses. You won't be able to see if these portions of your brain (located at the back of your head in your occipital lobes) aren't operating. Even if your eyes function properly, you won't be able to see if a gunshot wound or a stroke has damaged your occipital lobes. Your occipital lobes, not your eyes, are the area of your brain that permits you to see.

Parts of your brain process information about your body sensations, thoughts, and so on to generate your emotional experience, much as your brain processes visual information. The amygdala is heavily engaged in producing and influencing the physical sensations that lead to feelings of fear and anxiety, but feeling emotions is dependent on areas of your brain that help you interpret that information so that you know what you are feeling. So, just as seeing things requires your occipital lobes to understand information from your eyes, feeling emotions requires various areas of your brain to recognise and interpret these emotions. While the amygdala plays a role in some parts of your anxiety experience, you truly feel anxiety and fear due to several brain processes that bring emotions into consciousness. If you want to be neurologically right, you may think of the amygdala as the source of fear and anxiety, but it's not the only structure involved in our conscious experience of these emotions.

Designed To Feel Dread-Full

While the FFF response represents the amygdala's defence response, keep in mind that the emotional reaction we're feeling is a completely separate process. Often, the emotion is a sense of imminent danger or dread, which is commonly referred to as anxiety. Panic is a scary sensation that comes with extremely high levels of anxiety. Anxiety is meant to be uncomfortable to urge us to take action powerfully. In other words, it's an uneasy feeling that requires our attention to be drawn to a possible threat. Anxiety is a dreadful emotion that motivates us to try whatever to alleviate it. It is frequently the underlying cause of obsessing, fretting or engaging in obsessive activities. Anxiety can inspire these ideas and behaviours, while anxiety reduction can reward obsessive behaviours.

Anxiety makes us feel as though there is something wrong with ourselves. This isn't a hunch that something isn't right. We have the impression that something awful has occurred, is occurring, or will occur. The sensation is palpable and unavoidable. Often, friends or relatives will try to convince us that the feelings we are experiencing are not genuine. That couldn't be farther from the truth. When you feel anxiety or fear, you are experiencing a very real and extremely unpleasant emotional reaction, as well as physiological changes in your body. We don't want to downplay the fact that you're having a painful emotional reaction. But keep in mind that even if you have a strong sensation that you are in danger, it is still possible that you are not. The sensation does not properly represent actual danger; rather, the amygdala reacts as though there is danger. This is a very important piece of information to remember.

You may think of it like this: The amygdala functions similarly to an alarm system in your body, but the alert is not shown by a flashing light on the dashboard or a sound from a smoke detector. Emotion is being conveyed as communication. Instead of viewing a warning sign, you have a direct feeling that there is a risk. People who suggest you should just ignore the emotion don't realise it's not as simple as ignoring a flashing dashboard light or a beeping smoke detector. This is a feeling—the emotion you'd get if you thought a smoke detector was signalling a fire, rather than the sound of the smoke detector itself. The sensation is considerably more difficult to dismiss since it is a very clear indicator that you are in danger. When obsessions keep repeating themselves, and you can't let them go, the compelling feeling of anxiety comes into play, making you feel as though you need to focus on those obsessions. When you try to resist the compulsion, anxiety rises to an unbearable level, and when you fulfil the compulsion, the anxiety disappears. Many features of OCD are fuelled by anxiety. However, no matter how real the sense of worry is, it might be mistaken.

When teachers convey this point to college students, they explain that when it is incorrect, they might suffer worry. "Are you ever really nervous before an exam and end up getting a good grade?" is a typical example. Students begin to realise that worry and dread are not always predictive of what will occur. You can be terrified if you don't know where your vehicle keys are, worrying that you won't be able to find them, that you'll be late for work, that you'll miss an important meeting, and so on. Then you discover your keys in your coat pocket. The FFF response's sensations of fear and anxiety do not anticipate what will happen. They are genuine emotions, but they are not always reliable forecasts.

As you start to know the amygdala, you realise how frequently it may be reacting incorrectly—we may be approaching a bit of vine rather than a snake. However, it is simple to be duped into believing sensations of fear, worry, or dread. Even when we understand that the object is not a snake and feel relieved, the FFF response does not go away instantly. The consequences of the released adrenaline, elevated heart rate, and muscular tension might last for a long time. What are you going to make of that? You're still experiencing the impacts of the FFF reaction in your body for several minutes, so convincing yourself that you're safe might be tough.

We may learn to feel anxiety differently if we remind ourselves what it is: our brain's interpretation of a set of physiological reactions built on centuries of human experience when fighting and escaping were necessary, but which don't necessarily imply danger. This is especially essential if your obsessive thoughts or anxieties are related to bodily sensations or your health. Nicole, for example, has problems breathing when she is anxious, and when her breathing is off, she is frightened to drive because she is afraid she may pass out behind the wheel. She knew she wouldn't pass out once she learned her breathing problems were part of the FFF reaction. Nicole discovered that once she got in the car and started driving, she could forget about her breathing and focus on getting to her destination, especially if she switched on the radio and listened to an engaging morning program. If she hadn't understood the FFF reaction, she wouldn't have had the confidence to ignore her concerns about her breathing and get into the automobile.

It is critical to understand how we perceive the bodily feelings of the FFF reaction. We feel the impacts of adrenaline, muscular tension, or stomach distress when we encounter this protective reaction. But we are not having a heart attack or a stroke. We are neither insane nor out of control. Also, even though we are having a terrible emotional reaction, we are not necessarily in danger and should not believe that tragedy will soon befall us—even if that is how it seems. Of course, this is easier said than done, but it helps to recall that many times when you felt this way, everything ended out alright, despite your body's warnings.

Hopefully, you're learning more about your own physical and emotional sensations due to understanding how they're generated in the brain. First, you can see that these sensations are created by a portion of your brain over which you have no direct control and that this part of your brain may cause changes in your body that result in physical and emotional reactions based on information that you may not be aware of. Second, you may be able to perceive these bodily and emotional reactions in a new light once you realise that they serve the goal of assisting you in escaping or combating danger. You can also understand that you shouldn't rely on your feelings to warn you that awful things will happen.

Before you think you'd be better off without the amygdala, realise that its purpose is to protect you, even if it isn't always correct about whether something is harmful. And, now and again, you have to flee or fight to protect yourself, even if (glad) this is no longer the norm in the modern world. Remember that the amygdala generates certain pleasant feelings as a result of association-based learning. For example, you may have things in your home that appear little but that you treasure, such as Catherine's old wooden-handle potato masher, which she links with Sunday dinners at her grandmother's house. The amygdala is also responsible for the good sensations connected with old high school jerseys, which many former high school players keep long after the specifics of their winning seasons have faded.

In summary, you've learned that the amygdala, a brain defender, has been a part of the human experience since ancient times. You've probably heard that the amygdala has a defence response system that can take control of both your brain and your body if it believes you're in danger. You've learned that when your body produces the defence response, it also produces emotional emotions that might be upsetting. But you've also learned that the amygdala isn't always right, in part because it makes fast decisions based on limited information. While this technique may have safeguarded our forefathers and may occasionally come in handy for us, it does not always appear to match our twenty-first-century environment. The more you understand the processes that occur in your amygdala, the more you'll be able to comprehend why anxious sensations might develop when they aren't essential. Your anxiety experience may alter as you become more conscious and attentive to how your amygdala reacts. Furthermore, because the amygdala is the foundation of fear and anxiety in the brain, you may learn techniques to calm your amygdala to generate less defensive reaction and experience less worry. You will have fewer obsessions and will be better able to resist compulsions if you have less anxiety.

5

Let's Do This! The Secrets

THIS CHAPTER IS about figuring out how to deal with unwelcome toxic thoughts, whether they come as a result of a recent trigger or merely appear out of nowhere. Your attitude regarding these ideas makes all the difference, and the effective attitude is known as acceptance. This chapter explains acceptance and what it does not entail and offers practical strategies for obtaining it.

As previously mentioned, the anguish caused by toxic thoughts and the battle to deal with them tends to strengthen and stickier them over time. However, repetition becomes dull in most cases, and we become accustomed to it and stop paying attention. So why don't you get accustomed to having these thoughts? We've all been told that facing your worries would make them go away and that exposure is what helps. If you are frightened of elevators, ride them repeatedly until you are no longer afraid of them. If you are frightened of public speaking, enrol in a weekly course that will teach you how to do it. So, why doesn't this work for negative, toxic thoughts?

The issue is that exposure must be done correctly. Otherwise, it might have the reverse impact, empowering and reinforcing invasions. The exposure that is done correctly must be voluntary and without struggle. Many commonplace strategies that appear to be helping you deal in the present do not apply to these circumstances.

Your fight with intrusive thoughts, in particular, is what keeps them coming back. As a result, despite your greatest efforts, you are exacerbating the situation.

There is a distinction to be made between managing with each undesirable intrusive thought as it arises and beginning on a program to get rid of them. You're reading this book because toxic thoughts are ruining your life (or the life of someone you care deeply about). So, when each unwanted idea clogs your head, you want to know what to do right now. That method makes great sense, and in this chapter, I'll show you how to deal with each unwelcome intrusive idea as it arises. People have found this to be quite beneficial because, as mentioned in prior chapters, normal coping strategies frequently only strengthen the next intrusive idea.

When you're merely attempting to make the best of each intrusive thought, your objective is to get through that specific episode of intrusions with as little pain and anguish as possible. Learning to deal better with the next one is secondary to the primary objective of simply surviving the event. As a result, long-term reform is frequently ineffective. You've already discovered that your previous coping strategies are ineffective in the long run since they generally entail attempting to avoid, reassure, rationalise, or fight with the thoughts. And each of these tactics strengthens the idea, making it more strong and frightening the next time it arises.

However, there is some good news for you. Every piece of knowledge you've gleaned so far has contributed to a shift in your viewpoint and comprehension of invasions. Every misconception about ideas you've debunked has influenced how you think about them. And you now realise why sensible solutions to problems exacerbate the situation.

This chapter has two objectives: first, to give a better way of dealing each time you have an intrusive idea, and second, to retrain your brain. These two collaborate. As you learn to cope better, you begin the process of retraining your brain to be less frightened.

Dealing With Negativity - The Secrets

Are you more of a "glass half full" or "glass half empty" person? You might believe either way, but if you are a pessimist, you can perceive the world as a glass half empty. Negativity is a way of viewing the world characterised by the ideas and sentiments that a person displays about reality. Negative thought originates within a person. When you think negatively, you will only focus on the negative aspects of life and will not reflect enough positive. As a consequence, you will imagine the worst-case scenario for an action or decision. Negative individuals are dubious of whatever advice they are offered, and they do not trust others because of their prior experiences.

Even if a person adopts a negative mentality, it is unhealthy and impairs one's capacity to build meaningful connections with others. Do you prefer to look on the bright side of things, or do you usually find reasons to whine and complain? If you are optimistic, you will positively perceive things. However, if you are a pessimist, you will only perceive the bad aspects of every scenario.

When confronted with a problem or hardship, a negative person will instinctively default to a pessimistic forecast of what will happen in a particular circumstance.

Where Do You Get Negative Thoughts From?

Negative ideas originate in our minds from various sources, including the patterns of belief that we build through time. Money job, relationships, jobs, and other things may all be considered values. If you want to figure out where your negative ideas are coming from, you should ask yourself some probing questions.

1. Do you have a habit of complaining about everything?
2. Do you blame others before you blame yourself?
3. Do you enjoy predicting a bad conclusion in each given situation?

. . .

In addition to these fundamental issues, consider the factors that lead to your negative thinking, such as criticism of others, feeling victimised by various events, experiencing sadness, and always anticipating an emergency. When you consider these principles, you understand how rapidly bad thoughts may spread like wildfire.

You are more likely to think badly when you are in the presence of folks who always think negatively. The more you associate with individuals who have a pessimistic outlook on life, the more pessimistic you will become. As a result, it is critical to select companions that can lift you rather than those who continuously knock others down.

Having Negative Thoughts In Your Life

When you think negatively, it has a detrimental influence on your entire health. Your negative beliefs will cause your brain to go into survival mode, causing you to feel worried in every scenario that arises. When a person is subjected to prolonged stress, the psychological consequences are felt. Whether you are conscious of it or not, those negative ideas will have an impact on your capacity to operate, and they will have long-term implications that might threaten your well-being. You could find yourself unable to eat much, or you might stress eating to deal with the issue. When you lose or gain weight, you most often cope with negative thoughts caused by physical stress.

Negativity may strain your relationships with family members, coworkers, and others in your network. When you choose to dwell in the bad parts of your life, others will follow you, and they will be judgmental and critical of the people they meet. Soon, everything falls like a domino, causing you to experience a great deal of stress and anxiety.

In addition to marital issues, negativity nearly always leads to depression, and depression hurts people's health and well-being. Furthermore, if you are among individuals who enjoy tearing others down, you will not want to be with them and would prefer to go alone. It is critical to surround yourself with individuals who may have a positive impact on your life.

Now that we've examined the origins of negativity, we can consider quitting being so negative and beginning to live a pleasant and positive life.

1. Get away from the negative individuals in your life.

Consider a person you know who is usually negative. Avoid conversing with them. Put some space between yourself and them. Don't spend too much time with them since you could be injured or go through some difficult moments if you do. It's best if you don't interact with them at all.

2. Don't be afraid to break connections with those that bring you down.

If you've been in relationships with negative individuals, you should break them up as quickly as possible. Do not enter into a relationship with someone who is constantly negative. It would help if you surrounded yourself with individuals who will lift you rather than bring you down. Make developing ties with this latter sort of individual a top priority.

3. Avoid getting into a fight with someone negative.

You will lose an argument if you engage in it with a negative person. It'll be like something out of a movie, and you don't want to watch Mount Vesuvius erupt in front of you. Instead of interacting, walk away from the issue and return when the individual is ready to chat. Allow that individual some time to recover from whatever is bothering them.

4. Surround yourself with positive individuals.

You will feel happier and less melancholy if you surround yourself with positive individuals. Being around individuals like this will make you feel wonderful. You will also benefit from the outcome.

5. Substitute good thoughts for negative ones.

It is all very easy for us to fall into negative thought patterns that generate tension and anxiety. We must train ourselves to replace negative ideas with good ones. We must not allow ourselves to become engulfed in a whirlwind of negative ideas. Positive ideas should dominate your mind. Discover the incredible power of positive thought. It will have a positive impact on your entire day and make you feel a lot better as a consequence. For example, perhaps you despise going to work on Mondays and avoid it like the plague. Instead of concentrating on a potentially unfavourable scenario, you may say, "I'm looking forward to coming into work today because I'll be able to have my coffee, complete my work, and spend time with my favourite coworker." It will make a significant difference in your entire perspective if you can have just one optimistic idea.

6. Put a stop if you notice yourself heading off into the negative zone.

The next step is to recognise when you feel yourself falling into negative terrain. Keep an eye on yourself so that you don't fall into the habit of dwelling on the bad aspects of your life. For example, you may become melancholy due to constantly watching the news and witnessing the next tragedy. After seeing such an occurrence, your mind defaults to a gloomy frame of mind, and you believe that a catastrophic circumstance is just around the corner.

7. Don't complain.

It would help if you ceased complaining about whatever is going wrong whenever you find yourself doing so. Keep the thought in mind, and then go on with your life. You should not focus on the bad and consider all of the problems in your life. The fact is that complaining will do nothing to improve your situation. It will just make you feel worse. Complaining diverts your attention away from the things you desire.

8. Do not engage in office gossip with your coworkers.

Many of us engage in gossip with others. It's contagious, and it's causing havoc on workplaces and schools. It is not beneficial to you or anybody else in your life. You should stay away from it as much as possible. Gossip can devastate communities, causing distrust and a variety of other problems.

9. Don't attempt to read people's minds.

We may often find ourselves wishing we could read other people's minds to learn what they truly think of us. We also anticipate the worst from their thinking. It is essential to cease believing that those around you have negative sentiments about you. This will increase your tension and anxiety levels. It would help if you also quit thinking negatively. Do not jump to conclusions straight away; instead, be cool and relaxed.

10. Stop reading the news or using your Facebook account.

The news stream is one of the most dismal sources of information in our life, but we tend to absorb a lot of it this way. We go online to the BBC to learn about the current incident in Somalia or other events worldwide. Bad news might make us worry and have negative sentiments about things, which can impact our health. We would do well to avoid dealing with media that have particularly negative effects on our mental health. The same could be said about Facebook, which promotes false news and news stories that make us envy others and want what they have. These sources of information appear to bring us greater tension and concern. The best piece of advice is to avoid going to these areas. Stop watching the news and constantly reading through your Facebook page, which only contributes to your misery and unhappiness in life. Simply uninstall

Facebook. Deactivate your account and solely connect with your pals using Messenger.

Case Study

Chris used to be a pessimist. He was often complaining about little matters, such as the weather outdoors and the harsh work environment he was in. Even on good days, he found something to complain about. Chris quickly became the talk of the office, and he was named "Negative Ned." His employees used to tease him, which irritated him tremendously. He internalised these events, became unhappy, and beat himself up at home. This caused him to cry himself to sleep every night.

Chris was a man who kept his emotions to himself, and if he felt terrible, he didn't tell anyone. He did, however, display his negative attitude at work. His negativity made him anxious, and his blood pressure and pulse rate increased with each passing day. Chris realised he needed money even if he didn't like his work. He was still in denial about his negative problem. He was always certain that he could handle the problem on his own, but he ended up denigrating everyone around him. These folks also attempted to draw him into their own negative circle, so they became like-minded individuals. The entire workplace eventually became bored of everything and began criticising and tearing one other down. As a result, the workplace became unpleasant, and no one was having a productive time there.

Looking at this circumstance, we can observe that negativity breeds more negativity. When one apple goes rotten, it causes every other apple to become bad. Chris was a Negative Ned who struggled to connect with people. As a result, he erected a formidable barrier of animosity between himself and others. He grumbled about several things going on at work, and it became a habit for him. Then everyone around him began to complain about him. It contaminated everything in its path. Let's go back to the beginning of the narrative.

The situation had deteriorated to the point that coworkers were turning on each other, resulting in even more strife. As a result, additional coworkers were fired or forced to leave. Chris was likewise dismissed and had to leave because a group of coworkers eventually discovered something unacceptable in his work that was sufficient justification to terminate him. Chris, on the other hand, felt sad after being dismissed and seeking mental assistance. He was subsequently put on antidepressants for a while to cope with the problem. He saw a doctor, and received therapy for his depression. "Why don't you give giving optimism a chance?" his therapist said. Today, think positively." "Sure, why not?" Chris said.

Chris gave it his best try; he tried to be optimistic that day. He took his therapist's instructions and tried to be cheerful and grateful for his life. It made a significant impact. He still had a gripe about the weather or other work-related issues at the end of his first day at his new job. The next day, though, he understood that he had plenty to be thankful for and that he could count his blessings.

Chris thought to himself, "I feel so fortunate to be alive today. I have a wonderful therapist who has assisted me in making positive changes in my life. I adore my wife and two children, who have helped me get through this difficult time. What else could I want? I feel very grateful and overjoyed!" He also understood he was better than most others, which gave him the courage to claim he could be happy. He also saw how he might be more satisfied with what he had. Chris began to smile more frequently as time went on. He'd burst into spasms of laughter. There was a catharsis in some way, and he was releasing the tension and worry that had held him a prisoner for a long time. Everyone observed how much of a nice life Chris was having and wanted to live the same way he did. He'd found a much better job with greater perks at a larger firm in a big metropolis concerning his employment status. It had been his ideal job since he was a child.

The moral of this story is that you must overcome your negative ideas. To hear the good voice within you, you must block out all the bad voices in your brain and disregard everything that gets in your way. Chris's general morale and connection skills improved dramatically due to listening to the positive voice within him. People wanted to be closer to him and didn't want to push him away. Chris was also able to overcome his sadness and the need to take antidepressants, which had been his one-stop answer to all of his issues. Nonetheless, once he maintained a cheerful attitude for one day, it all led to his road of recovery and prosperity.

It is critical to realise how harmful negativity can be. It has the potential to infect your spirit as well as your bodily and mental well-being. We frequently find ourselves being judgmental, and it can be difficult to silence the inner critic within, but it must be taught. Being positive is one technique to quiet the negative voice inside of you. It enables you to enter a whole new world of positivity. It is critical to look for methods to be optimistic every day and find the bright side of things. When you can accomplish this, you will experience greater joy and serenity inside yourself. If you don't have a positive attitude, it may not be easy to find purpose in your life.

Furthermore, you must discover good things to be grateful for and stop wasting energy complaining about all the unpleasant aspects of life. The best approach to go is to make a positive move in the right direction. It would help if you approached life with pleasure and tranquillity to have a better and more positive life.

Enemies Of Acceptance

Three common reactions occur immediately following an incident of intrusive thoughts: **Guilt**, **Doubt** and **Urgency**. All of them are common. They often cause entanglement and contradictory effort, undermining one's capacity to execute the six stages outlined above. Understanding how these common emotions obstruct healing makes it simpler to practice acceptance when an unwelcome intrusive thought appears.

Guilt

Guilt (and the reassurance-seeking it frequently prompts) comes in the way of developing an accepting mindset. Some people feel a rush of guilt after having an incident of unwelcome intrusive thoughts. They then seek confirmation from others that they are not a horrible person or that their ideas have caused harm to others. This is referred to as externalising the comments. It implies you're acting out your internal dialogue between your

Worried, **False Comfort**, and **Wise Mind** voices with real people in your life. This is a type of reassurance-seeking in which you urge people to reassure you that your ideas are fine. And, like any comfort, it just gives brief respite while amplifying the intrusion's force.

Guilt may be connected with a wide range of disturbing ideas. Harmful or self-harming invasions might result in guilt. "What type of person do I think I am to think such a thing?" After experiencing blasphemous ideas, you may feel unholy or sinful. When you seek comfort from others in situations like these, you run the danger of adding to your guilt for upsetting or frightening them. You may also seek reassurance that having those negative thoughts does not reflect negatively on your character, reinforcing the voice of **False Comfort**. Keep in mind that your ultimate objective is to quiet **False Comfort**.

Here's an example of an internal commentary or dialogue in which someone is disputing with himself about unwelcome intrusive thoughts.

Worried Voice: Wise Mind says it's good to have these ideas, but I feel that "lusting in your heart" is just as terrible as doing it.

Worried Voice says you don't even attend church; what's the point of all this moralising? I questioned my priest, and he replied that everyone has terrible ideas; all you have to do is beg for forgiveness, and you will be forgiven.

Slow down, wise mind. I don't understand why I should seek forgiveness. That only applies when you have knowingly done something wrong, in a circumstance where you had a choice and chose wrongly. We are not liable for events that occur when we have no choice or control. It is just not true that we have control over what thoughts enter our minds. We have control over what we choose to do, but not over the intuitive ideas that arise.

Looking for reassurance while you are feeling guilty may make you feel better in the short term, but it adds to your suffering when you learn that it occasionally hurts or frightens others and eventually increases your Worried Voice. Much better to practice observing that sensations linked with your ideas will fade on their own if you leave them alone.

Doubt

When you experience an unwelcome toxic thought, you want to know for certain that there is no risk and that the intrusion will pass peacefully. Attempting to eliminate all uncertainties and ambiguity is a huge obstacle to achieving an accepting mindset. Everyone wants to be certain that not dealing with the notion is safe and that identifying it as a thought rather than an impulse is not harmful. You want to be confident that the notion is not a reflection of your personality and that you will not go insane or lose control. This is an understandable desire. Regrettably, it cannot be met.

The desire for assurance is a key element in the persistence of your unwelcome intrusive thoughts. And, come to think of it, where else would you want perfect certainty? Do you raise your car and have a qualified technician inspect the brakes, steering, and gearbox every time you go for a drive? Do you avoid walking on sidewalks because automobiles occasionally lose control and run over pedestrians? Do you require someone to taste your food before you eat it? Do you check in with your children every hour to see whether they still love you? Certainly not!

The issue is that unwelcome intrusive thoughts are so frightening. That's because nervous thinking takes over, and as repulsive as it may be, the thought seems to have a high likelihood of happening. Even though the likelihood is minimal, the repercussions of killing someone or throwing a child out the window are so huge and awful that the thought feels scary and dangerous.

False Comfort: Wise Mind, I need to find a better way to convince Worried Voice that the ideas don't matter, but no matter what I say, it keeps asking the same question again and over.

Wise Mind: The issue is that thinking Worried Voice is reassuring. What-ifs will always arise. Worried voice must accept that it cannot offer 100 per cent assurance. We don't have any genuine assurance about anything.

False Comfort: But if I don't soothe Worried Voice, it worsens and becomes furious with me.

Wise Mind: Tell Worried Voice that you love it, but if you continue to reassure it, it will never learn how to live with uncertainty, which is something we all need to learn.

Seeking external comfort is another stage in the counterproductive pursuit of certainty. People are seeking external reassurance to ease their anxieties once more. Frequently, their friends and relatives offer false assurance to keep their loved ones comfortable at the moment or encourage them to stop seeking reassurance. It doesn't last more than a few minutes of relief. This type of exchange is not beneficial.

Self: Tell me you're confident the plane won't crash while you're on board. I keep thinking about it, and it feels like a forewarning.

Don't be ridiculous, family member. I assure you that I will be alright. I'll call you when I arrive.

But you can't be sure, can you? Please do not leave. I'm receiving a message here.

Planes are safe, according to a family member.

Self: Okay, but you must contact me as soon as you arrive. I'll be worrying about you the entire time.

Sometimes the urge for reassurance becomes so intense that you become addicted to it. If you consider yourself a reassurance addict, try the following strategy: Set up a weekly "ration" of reassurances for yourself.

Assume that reassurance is prohibitively expensive and that your budget is limited. Only use it when it appears to be essential. It might be the first step in breaking the reassurance habit.

This is significantly different from the usual comfort and encouragement that individuals seek and get in their daily lives. True reassurance occurs only once, it is effective, and the problem is resolved. It is not an unanswerable question or a false promise.

Urgency

As previously said, every unwelcome intrusive idea is accompanied by a sense of urgency. Giving in to that sense of hurry leads you astray from the therapeutic attitude of acceptance. We understand that each incursion appears to suggest an emergency (or an impending disaster) and that you must act promptly. However, this is a false alarm. When you are bluffed or deceived by this false alarm, you will expend energy attempting to silence it, encountering the repercussions of paradoxical effort, unwittingly increasing entanglement. Urgency makes you feel as though matters must be addressed right now rather than later. It makes it difficult to pause before classifying, rise above the noise, accept and allow, and allow time to pass. In reality, a sense of urgency works against every necessary step in dealing with unwelcome intrusive thoughts. There is a link between being concerned by uncertainty and having a sense of urgency. If something is ambiguous or unknown, there is a strong desire to resolve it as soon as possible.

If you seek aid from family and friends, they may begin to feel that you are in an emergency as well, reinforcing the impression that you must act immediately. They think of everything False Comfort has previously attempted.

Slowing down, floating above the fray, and practising letting time pass are the most effective ways to deal with a sense of urgency.

You now have an attitude and a method for coping with unwelcome intrusive ideas and toxic thoughts that appear out of nowhere. This technique and attitude foster a fresh viewpoint and, in the long run, will considerably lessen your distress. Avoiding anxiety traps and hijackings, as well as learning these new approaches, will require practice. But don't give up hope: this method has helped hundreds of individuals who, like you, were overwhelmed and at a loss for what to do. You've already learned a lot and made big improvements. The next chapter presents a strategy for developing new brain circuitry so that undesirable ideas lose their strength and cease troubling you at all.

6

How To Accept Yourself

THE SECRET to accepting yourself the way you are is to understand and actively control the way your brain functions. This will change how undesirable thoughts feel, and they will ultimately cease bugging you. What you've discovered so far whilst reading this book is that your normal method of dealing with unwelcome intrusive thoughts does not work. In reality, it accomplishes the reverse, trapping your brain, body, and ideas within their current cycle. We've discussed how an accepting attitude allows changes to occur, and in this chapter, we set out a plan of purposeful activities to make that happen.

There is a consensus that the most effective method to alter your brain and overcome unwanted intrusive thoughts is to allow yourself to think your fearful ideas on purpose. In other words, you are purposefully exposing yourself to concepts while developing new and better techniques to regulate your emotions. You rewire your brain and produce long-term changes when you take control of your experience rather than being inundated by it. This is known as exposure practice.

Acceptance is required to reap the greatest benefits from exposure work. Indeed, exposure work without acceptance is a formula for pain and ineffectiveness. It is vital to be uncomfortable, but understanding how exposure works may provide you with additional drive and bravery. This will lay the groundwork for future practice optimisation.

Forgiving The Past

It might be difficult to forgive individuals and events that have profoundly wounded us in the past. However, we must learn to forget the past and find methods to forgive the injuries that have given us so much pain. We must devise strategies for overcoming our varied conditions and forgiving the past.

It's easier said than done. However, it is something that you must do to free yourself of the emotional and psychological baggage that you have accumulated in your life. Perhaps you have had a breakup with someone. It was a terrible experience for you; you're trying to find out how to move on, but it's gnawing at you all the time. That is where you must learn to let go and forgive yourself for the numerous things you may have gone through in the past to move on to the things that motivate you.

Forgiving previous errors, misjudgments, and heartbreaks can allow you to conquer your anxieties and achieve inner peace. You're bothered by what's going on in the world at times. Some things might make you anxious and stressed because they remind you of childhood trauma or other tough experience in the past. When this happens, you begin to experience the traumatic events of your past.

It would help if you learned to forgive yourself for your mistakes in the past. It is not going to happen by itself. Often, forgiveness is a lengthy procedure that must be completed before it can be carried out. The only way to move on is to forget what occurred. To be sure, it may take you years to recover from the pain that someone has caused you, and you may spend a lifetime attempting to forgive them. The sooner you accomplish this. However, the better off you will be.

There are many examples of people who have carried the emotional baggage of childhood trauma throughout their lives. The actor, Robin Williams, who had a lonely upbringing, is one such example. His parents confined him to the house's attic, where he was forced to play with his toys by himself. Except for intimate dinner events, he rarely visited his parents. In such a situation, Robin felt as though he was always seeking the approval and love of others. Many people loved Robin and showed it, but he struggled to love himself because he hadn't felt that way as a child. As a result, he struggled with the thought of love throughout his life because his parents had not given him love. That deep grief followed him to his death in 2014, when he committed suicide.

Robin Williams exemplifies someone who has had childhood anxieties, and struggles follow him throughout his life. He could never forgive and forget the past, even though it would have allowed him to live a more fulfilled life. We may learn from this example that childhood fears and trauma can accompany us into adulthood and may follow us to death if we are not careful. Because our problems are hidden deep within us, it might not be easy to express them to others. There are wounded children inside our psychology who are trying to overcome the problems of the past, but the sooner we can conquer the past, the sooner we will be joyful and able to enjoy a life full of love, joy, serenity, and good fortune.

Will Hunting from the 1997 film **Good Will Hunting** (starring Ben Affleck, Matt Damon, and Robin Williams) is another example of someone who had to let go of the past. Will, played by Matt Damon, is the main character whose past has been haunted because he was abandoned by his parents and has lived as an orphan with no relatives. He attempted to hide his fears by drinking, smoking cigarettes, and committing physical violence against others. He did, however, meet Dr Maguire, a psychologist portrayed by Robin Williams. Will was able to connect on a deep emotional level with the psychologist, who provided him with the assistance he needed to overcome his prior trauma. In one emotionally charged scene, Robin Williams extracted all of Matt Damon's character's pain by breaking into tears and holding him. Maguire, Robin's character, kept telling him, "It's not your fault." It was useful to see this moment because it demonstrated that the past could be successfully forgiven and wiped clean if a person desired to do so. Maguire was able to extract Will's pain and get him to the point of forgiveness for the past. Will would be able to go on and do what he was supposed to do, which was "go and see about a lady," even though he would never forget what his parents had done to mistreat him and finally leave him. The moving narrative demonstrated how the past might be forgotten for a person to move forward and seek his destiny. Will would be able to leave behind the darkness of his past and follow his desire of finding love with someone if he had moments of healing and completeness.

What can we do to forgive ourselves? The essential thing to remember is that we require healing—spiritual, emotional, and bodily health. Our emotions and thoughts are not in the proper place. We have been harmed in the past, and we believe it is a black pit from which we cannot escape. However, we must bring ourselves to repentance for our own errors and the things that have brought us sorrow and worry, as well as forgiving those around us who have wounded us in some manner. It is not an easy route, but it is well worth taking since it will allow us to discover a way to feel better and recover. It is a lifelong process in some situations, but as we let go of our extra emotional baggage, we may see a more liberated and wealthy future in our thoughts. We must let go of tension, anxiety, and other stumbling blocks. If we don't, we may be clinging to something for the rest of our lives that will eventually lead to our own death and destruction, like in Robin Williams's case.

LET's have a look at how we can do this. How do we emotionally let go of the past in our hearts and minds?

Practical Applications

1. Make a list of everything that is giving you concern and stress and save it for later. Allowing yourself to unleash all of your pain onto the page is a good idea. The paper is then burned, torn, or otherwise destroyed to demonstrate that it is no longer there.

. . .

2. Express your regret to those you have offended. You must do with this application to express your regret to those you may have caused grief and distress. You may not know how much this has affected your connection, and you will have to take the initiative because the other person is unlikely to take the first move. You must be proactive in this regard.

3. Stay so busy that you don't have time to worry or reflect on the past. You should find ways to keep yourself occupied so that you don't dwell on the past. Do a variety of tasks that will allow you to find joy and significance in your life. Do activities that excite you.

4. Spend time with the individuals you care about and avoid negative ones. Another thing to consider is spending time with individuals who make you happy and avoiding Negative Nancys and other people who will only bring you down. This will assist you in living a happier life.

Case Study

Frank had a traumatic experience in the past that he could not forget. In a one-sided romance with a female, he was severely upset. It was tough since she had cheated on him, requiring him to end the relationship. For years, he searched for and attempted to overcome his pain, but every time he tried dating, the subject came up again, and he could sense that he was suffering from it on an ongoing basis. Then he went to his mentor and revealed everything that had been holding him back. He cried in his arms, freed of the burden of how painful this event had been for him. It was tough, but Frank was able to overcome his feelings of guilt and unforgiveness. He let all of that go out of his life. And after he'd accomplished that, he thought he could genuinely be free—free, at long last.

To break the chains of tyranny from the past, you must learn to forgive and release the things of the past. It is not simple, but you will find yourself in a better emotional, spiritual, and physical state once accomplished.

Looking On The Bright Side Every Day

Being optimistic has a lot of power. Being optimistic may have a significant influence on the lives of others. On Monday, you get up and say to yourself, "I can do it! I'm looking forward to starting a fresh day at work. It's going to be fantastic. I bathed and drank my coffee. I'm ready to go now."

When you recognise that you can make a big difference in the world, you will alter your attitude and expectations. Consider this: our lives are too short to be concerned with trivial and hollow concerns. We should not go about our days complaining about everything that happens to us. To be sure, there are many things worth grumbling about, such as a meal that takes too long to cook at a restaurant or office gossip, among other things. We might easily become depressed and complain about these things. As a result, we aim to walk you through each stage of building a good attitude and altering your response to various events in your life.

The first thing you must realise is that life is full of unpleasant and demanding situations. Nothing truly valuable will come easily. Sometimes you have to tough it out to feel better about your life. To achieve your objectives, you must constantly put in a lot of effort and dedication. And we frequently fail to achieve our objectives because we are depressed due to all the expectations we place on ourselves or others. In the midst of all of this, we are concerned with achieving our ambitions and objectives. When you have an ultimate goal in sight, you can go forward with your life and get one step closer to the turning point in your life. Perhaps you aim to save £3,000 for your next trip, or you want to get healthy and work out to combat sadness and live a healthier lifestyle. Perhaps you want to pay off a college loan, so you put in the extra effort. Sometimes we just need to be more direct about our objectives because we can only have more reasonable expectations of those who will lead us ahead.

You may be asking how you may get into a good frame of mind. It's actually a lot simpler than you would imagine. The first thing you should do is get a pen and paper and jot down fifteen things you are grateful for. When you gain a sense of what makes you appreciative, you will notice what impacts your thinking.

One of the most effective things you can do in your life is to practice appreciation. It can assist you in getting out of a rut when you're stuck and unable to go forward. Furthermore, it aids in the recovery from depression when you are faced with the loss of a job or another disaster that throws you a curveball. As a result, you may feel powerless or heartbroken. However, when you write down what you are grateful for, you will realise how lucky you are and how glad you may be. Life is a valuable gift. When you consider how many items have been given to you, you realise that you have the support of many people who want to help you move out of your problems and into a more prosperous life. Consider the individuals who care about you, such as your friends, parents, siblings, and others. Consider your financial position as well as the work you go to every day. Consider these privileges and let go of any sense of entitlement that you may have toward them. It would help if you understood that you are given far more than you deserve and that everything is a gift of grace. Instead of complaining about the lack of funds in your bank account, take a minute to offer thanks to someone who has impacted your life for the better. Believe that it will transform your day for the better.

Stop right now and get a pen and a piece of paper. Make a list of the things you're grateful for.

Now that you've taken that first step, you can look back and see that you're well on your path to being a more optimistic person. Consider a period when you earned achievement. Perhaps you had an A in calculus in high school even though you disliked math but enjoyed studying it. Perhaps you won a top-tier internship at a Fortune 500 firm during your undergraduate years, which led to full-time employment there. Perhaps you were able to recover from a long-standing psychiatric condition. You experienced miraculous healing. Be appreciative of the moments that have passed and how you have conquered various challenges. Consider how strong you have grown due to conquering all of the hardships that have come your way. Not everyone can fight the good battle in the manner that you have. Having diverse psychological and physical illnesses may be difficult, and when you are sad, simply getting out of bed can be difficult. Once you've gotten over a major setback, you may realise that you did a good job and rejoice.

Become Your Own Positive Hero

You are ready to improve the world now that you have a thankful mentality, and one of the finest ways to do so is to help others. More than anything else, helping others may enhance your moods and attitude. For example, if you assist an old lady in loading her groceries into her car and moving the cart away, you have done something to assist someone else. This can boost your self-esteem and make you feel better.

Helping others is a type of therapy that allows you to make a big difference in the lives of others while simultaneously improving your emotional well-being. When you cultivate a positive mentality, you may make a significant difference in the lives of others. You might, for example, smile at yourself in the mirror and say to yourself, "See, you're doing very great! You're going to have a fantastic day!" Then you'll feel instantly better. It fills you with pleasant vibes, which allows you to keep going in your mind.

When you laugh, the positive hero mentality becomes even more powerful. When you deliver a joke and make others laugh, or when you watch Robin Williams or another comic on Netflix and laugh your head off, you may quickly fill a space with positivity and combat negative sentiments. All of these will make you feel more optimistic and help you to perform at your best. You should be able to be happy, playful, and appreciative all at the same time. Being a positive hero may transform you into a beacon of light amid the darkness that pervades our existence. As previously said, there is much to be upset and worried about in this world; but, you may rectify by making the world a better place by adding pieces of positivity, making others laugh and smile, and occasionally giving them a high-five. It will transform your entire perspective and bring you the joy you never knew you possessed.

We are not attempting to paint the scene entirely in brilliant colours. It might not be easy to maintain a cheerful attitude at times. It would help if you suffered greatly in this life from the anxieties and worries of ordinary daily routine. Some days, you may lie in bed and wonder to yourself, "Why should I deal with all of this?" "I'm not looking forward to going to work today." But what if I told you that it is possible to overcome your severe self-doubt and begin living each day in a more optimistic and cheerful mindset? You've got this! I'm confident you can.

Case Study

Emma was having difficulty concentrating in class. She failed her science test and struggled to find the motivation to prepare for subsequent tests. The girl was concerned about her chances of getting into a top institution despite her low marks. She realised she wasn't outstanding in the sciences, and she began to feel guilty and concerned about her future. Things had become so terrible that she couldn't even get out of bed in the morning because she was so anxious.

Emma was then required to attend a counsellor about her difficulties. Her name was Dr Rachel, and she was an exceptionally gifted therapist. She made Emma establish a goal to break free from the negative and depressing cycles in her life by attempting to earn a C in her science class and obtaining tutoring to assist her in boosting her mark. Emma felt better and knew that this strategy would benefit her. Megan, her tutor, helped her. They worked together to improve Emma's scientific study abilities. Megan was a good influence in Emma's life, and she told her, "Emma, I know you're doing your best. Continue to do so. Recognise that you can do everything you set your mind to. It is not impossible. I know you can do so much better, and I know you will." Megan taught Emma a lot of positive self-talk, which helped her a lot, especially while she was going through difficult times in her life.

Emma received 60 per cent on her test after that period. Instead of telling herself things like, "You're an idiot. "Get down on your knees and scream your heart out!" she told herself, "It's okay, Emma. You had a rough ride, but you can do better the next time. You can perform a better job if you study harder and smarter. But you should also seek assistance." Emma acquired a can-do attitude by embracing a development mentality. She obtained the C she sought with Megan's assistance, especially after Megan had consistently encouraged and supported her. Everything worked out nicely, and Emma improved her self-confidence and self-talk, which helped her achieve.

How To Be More Positive

Let's have a look at how you can put what we've discussed in this chapter into practice. Let's go over the many things you may do to cultivate a happy mentality.

1. Surround yourself with positive people all of the time.

This is the one that is relevant to the case study we just discussed. When you surround yourself with positive people, you feel better and have a more optimistic outlook on life. By focusing on them rather than on negative individuals, you will feel better and begin to feel more cheerful. This is necessary for you to achieve more satisfaction, and you will no longer be concerned about what others think of you.

2. Take up a pastime or sport that offers you joy and allows you to do whatever you want in life.

Find a pastime or sport that you enjoy and participate in it, ideally with others. You may, however, bike it alone if you like. Hang out with individuals who share your interests so that you may have fun achieving your objectives together and having a good time in general. This generates good energy, which will bring more joy into your life.

3. Give yourself a compliment or two every day.

This is a critical step in your rehabilitation. It would help if you attempted to congratulate yourself at least once or twice a day. If you want to think positively, you must speak positively to yourself and work on your self-esteem and confidence. You will discover that the more self-affirmation you give yourself, the better you will look at yourself and have a brighter and more optimistic attitude. Look in the mirror and say to yourself, "You're great!" "You're a fantastic musician!" "You did an excellent job!" Make an effort to give yourself more compliments. You will notice that you will have greater self-assurance and confidence. It'll be fantastic.

4. Consider everything beautiful that has happened in your life. Remember the good old days.

Return to the wonderful memories you have stored in your memory and recall what caused you to delight in the past with more certainty. We frequently need to be reminded of the things we've gone through in our lives, even the previously tough things for us, but they turned out to be quite beneficial to us. It is critical to "let the happy moments roll" in our minds' camera so that we can remember all of the amazing experiences we have had in our lives and not concentrate on the unpleasant events that may have occurred.

5. Share your positive feelings.

Another thing you may do is communicate your happy feelings to others. This includes things like smiling, laughing, shaking hands, and even hugging. Positive emotions may make someone else's day and provide you joy as you've never felt before. It will have a significant impact on your life. It also lifts your spirits and allows you to connect with others, allowing everyone to feel happy.

6. Establish daily goals that you can meet.

It is critical to be goal-oriented in your life if you want to see worthwhile outcomes. An optimistic individual realises how much they want to accomplish more each day to pursue their goals and aspirations. Being optimistic can help you discover more joy and meaning in your life, which will boost your self-esteem, self-confidence, and image. And after you've accomplished your objectives, go out and celebrate. Pour yourself a drink of wine or a pint of beer to lift your spirits.

7. Stay away from multitasking.

We prefer to do multitask in modern culture, and it is detrimental to our health. Instead of focusing on one activity and executing it well, we end up performing several tasks poorly. The remedy is to quit multitasking and conduct a lot of "mono-tasking." It's a lot better now. You should avoid attempting to perform too many tasks at once. You'll only be able to perform a few things well at once. The more you pile on your plate, the more you'll feel overwhelmed and burdened by it all. And you certainly don't want it in your life. So stop opening 10 tabs on Google Chrome. Stop responding to SMS messages while attempting to work. It can be postponed. It can. Take it one step at a time. There will be a noticeable change.

8. Look for a greater calling and significance in your life.

Another thing you may do is to find meaning for everything in your life. To discover this purpose, you may go to religion, values, and ethics. Having a vocational purpose can assist you in being a happier and more productive person with much to give to this life. If you can look deeply into your life and ask yourself questions like, "Why am I here?" If you ask yourself, "What is my purpose?" you will be able to dig into life's questions with a curious mindset that will drive you to learn and improve. You may think about what you want to do in the future by philosophically examining all of the circumstances you've been in. It is really beneficial.

9. Forget the past and quit worrying over negative ideas.

Next, attempt to let go of past mistakes, relationships, and everything else holding you back from going ahead. It would help if you did not focus on the negative aspects of life but rather on the positive. Reflect on and cherish your successes, but don't get bogged down by previous guilt, mistakes, and other things that might bring you down. Instead, move on and quit worrying about it.

10. Imagine a wonderful future.

As you create a mindset that no longer turns to the past for validation, you will be able to look forward to the future. Consider all of the goals you want to achieve in your life. You could like to accomplish numerous activities, so select the excellent ones and do them. Consider future possibilities and have a growth mindset in which you are eager to learn from every circumstance and develop so that you may live in the future and perform an excellent job. You're going to be fantastic!

11. Eliminate activities from your life that aren't beneficial to you.

You should say no to everything that is just simple rubbish and will not add substantially to your life. This includes stuff you don't need to buy and junk food you want to eat. You want to avoid things that aren't beneficial to you, therefore do your best to avoid them.

12. Maintain a clean and well-organised home and workspace.

When you keep your house tidy and organised, you will feel

much better about yourself and everything in your home—nothing like a tidy house or workstation to make you feel good. You should be aware that doing so will improve your mood and make you feel your best.

13. Tell someone you adore them.

This is essential for maintaining a love circle. You should express your feelings for someone you care about, a close buddy, or a group. This covers both men and women. In this case, there should be no gender discrimination or homophobia. Love transcends all sexual aspects. It is about genuine love and friendship with people, and it is profound. When you tell someone you love them, you inject your body with a flood of good vibes. There is no greater set of words that touch your heart and give you goosebumps than to say, "I love you."

14. Recognise when you fall into a negative thinking habit and strive to break free from it.

One thing you should do is to observe your mental processes and notice if you begin to think negatively. Then it would help if you made an effort to do something about it. Don't just look into space. Act! Get something done. Get some exercise or do something useful. Get out of the house for a few minutes. Allow laziness to creep into your life and generate tension and anxiety. Instead, be proactive in combating the negative ideas that creep into your mind. Try to react aggressively so that you can complete everything on your to-do list.

15. Accept that you will have bad days and that this is normal.

You can't be happy every day. Now and then, let the negativity out. The last thing to remember is that you will not always be positive. It's natural to want to be pessimistic on certain days. However, it would help if you did not linger on it for too long. Get rid of any bad energy that has taken up home in your body and spirit right now. Could you give it to the wind? Let out some steam now and then. It's good for you. Please don't feel obligated to suppress it for an extended period. It would help if you got it out sooner rather than later. Try to fight any negativity inside yourself and develop a positive mentality that can transform the world.

Why Practicing This Will Help You In The Short Term And Long Term

It is critical to recognise that the road to being more optimistic is a process. It will not look the same for everyone. Some people will need a longer time to digest and recover from unpleasant events, but they can focus on becoming more optimistic after doing so. It requires time and effort. If you are used to being negative and concentrating on pessimistic ideas in your brain, it will take some time for you to have positive thoughts going through your head. Be kind to yourself. Recognise that things can and will change, but it will take time. Also, even if you are concerned about future events and possibilities, you should focus on the good. You will be happy if you look on the bright side of things.

Life is brief. We must seize every chance to find joy and purpose in our lives because that is what is essential. It's not about a huge fancy job, a lot of money, or a lot of goods. On the other hand, life is about enjoying the little everyday gifts that it has to give. That necessitates having a grateful heart, one that is eager to take in every moment and appreciate its goodness while making time to say "thank you." When you do this, you will feel a sense of freedom and excitement like you have never felt before. It will relieve you of all your worries and stress and bring you to a more enjoyable and prosperous future. It will be a wonderful experience for you.

7

When To Seek Help

So far, we've been discussing toxic thoughts that are frightening but not necessarily dangerous. They may be annoying, humiliating, or even embarrassing, but they are all occurrences that only live in your imagination. Despite your deep fears, you are unlikely to act on your dreams. As previously stated, they are the result of excessive control rather than a lack of control. They truly speak to the polar opposite of who you are because you fight the thoughts that are most unlike your character. They may seem weird, but they are not what you desire or want, even if you do it "unconsciously."

However, many types of ideas and preoccupations recur but have a distinct feel to them. If you find yourself recurring to the ideas mentioned in the following paragraphs, speaking with a mental health professional about them is advisable. There are just a few kinds of these thoughts, but you should be aware of them.

Invited Thoughts

Certain dreams, ideas, or pictures of self-destructive action might represent genuine desires to deal with unpleasant sensations or situations. People occasionally rely on them in times of difficulty, and they appear calming or comforting—as if they are escape plans if things get too difficult to bear. It is also possible that provoked thoughts of vengeance or anger develop into real intentions to hurt people. The following are some examples:

- If I can't handle it, I can always go drunk. So what; who gives a damn?
- If she abandons me, I can always leap off a building or shoot myself if I can't take it any longer. Then she'll be sorry.
- I deserve better treatment. Therefore I'll let the air out of his tyres. Allow him to ponder who did it and why. It will remain a well-guarded secret of mine.
- I'm going to harm her if she says it one more time.

If ideas or visions become real plans or acts harmful to others or self-harming, they do not qualify as unwanted intrusions and should be treated immediately.

Real Suicidal Preoccupations

The sensations produced by ideas are rarely pleasant for those who are sad or suffering. "This is not me; I enjoy my life, so why would I believe such a thing?" Instead, the sensation is a genuine want to die. It seems like this in innocuous unwanted intrusive thoughts: "What if, in a fit of madness, I murder myself when I don't really want to?"

With comparison, in severe depression, it looks like this:

- I don't know if I deserve to die or if I want to die.
- This is hopeless; my only alternative is to die.
- My family will be better off if I don't stay. They'll forgive me or put up with me after a while.
- I can't take it any longer. I must take severe action.

Although the idea returns, the sense of deserving to die is not the same as the worry that you could, despite your best efforts, do something detrimental to yourself. These ideas arise in the context of other symptoms of depression or bipolar disorder, such as lack of appetite, difficulty sleeping, loss of enjoyment, irritability, and feelings of worthlessness and hopelessness. Instead of being terrifying, the thought of death seems soothing or appropriate.

If Perspective Is Entirely Lost

You may read this book and have no idea what I'm saying or why I'm making the points I'm making. Or maybe you believe it's all nonsense. You may not be able to focus well enough to think clearly. And this isn't simply a passing emotion that lasts a few minutes, hours, or days, but something that seems to be ongoing. In such a scenario, reading this book will not give any answers, you must seek professional help immediately.

Hopelessness

A sense of hopelessness can sometimes be mistaken for reality. Even if the objective facts show that nothing is hopeless, dismal sentiments might occur. In reality, negative sentiments can occur in circumstances and situations that are easily curable. As we have explored in previous chapters, the battle against pessimism may sometimes seem more genuine. However, despairing thoughts might give you the erroneous impression that you have no other alternatives in life and that your life is finished. This notion may be repeated indefinitely. Following are some examples:

- Everything has gone wrong for me. My lover despises me, and I'll never be able to win him back. I'm failing school because I'm performing so poorly. Even my friends regard me as a loser and refuse to spend time with me. My life has ended.
- All of this serves no purpose. I am simply a loser.

If you genuinely cannot look past a sense of hopelessness, it is essential to seek professional assistance.

Agitation

Finally, rushing thoughts might seem like intrusive thoughts at times. However, racing thoughts are a hallmark of agitation linked to depression, bipolar disorder, or other medical problems. Racing thoughts tend to jump from issue to topic as if you can't finish one before the next appears.

This agitation is usually often accompanied by additional symptoms, such as an inability to enjoy life's pleasures (anhedonia) and early morning awakening (rising with a "start" in the middle of the night and then being unable to go back asleep). People's appetites for food, sex, and regular daily activities alter dramatically. You may be irritated, find it difficult to concentrate, and find it impossible to relax. Your sense of comedy may evolve. Because these sensations are so intense, agitation is sometimes mislabeled as acute anxiety, although it is a symptom of depression or a similar disease. It necessitates a distinct approach, which is frequently medical. It is quite curable.

You could read this chapter and say to yourself, "Yes, that's me." And, if you do, the best suggestion comes from a professional, not a self-help book.

However, you may question, debate, and worry about whether you fit into any of these categories, which is typical for anybody experiencing unwelcome toxic thoughts. After all, uncertainty is the fuel that drives worry. In reality, you are unlikely to fit into any of these categories, yet you will still profit much from this book.

8

Conclusion

As WE NEAR the end of our trip and attempt to defeat the demons inside us, we realise nothing to be concerned about. Life is brief and transient. We're living one minute, and the next, we're laying in our graves. I'm sure we'll regret the time we wasted thinking about our life before we die.

Because life is valuable, we should not squander our time in this world worrying about trivial matters. We don't always have it all together, and we occasionally break down and weep to let it all out, but it doesn't mean we stay there. Let go of the energy that is weighing you down. Stop worrying and get it all out. That is an important aspect of your future.

Releasing the negative energy inside you will be an essential element of being a more liberated person. By injecting optimism into your life, you may live with an open mind and heart that is eager to learn from all experiences. Try putting on a cheerful expression. Smile, but do so with purpose and joy. Then you'll be able to feel what it's like to have fewer worries in your life. Discover new ways to feel the delight that never fades. Even if you are not happy one day, you will always experience a profound feeling of pleasure knowing that you are creating a meaningful life for yourself on Earth and that you will not allow anything to bring you down.

This book has taken you through the actions you'll need to take to quit worrying in your life. First, we discussed the reasons for your mental congestion and what you might do to deal with various life events. We also presented several case studies that showed the difficulties and how they may be dealt with in the real world. We discussed doing less and worrying less, getting rid of the trash, waiting to respond to communications, and forgiving the past. Furthermore, we discussed many methods for coping with negative ideas that may arise and taking control of your mind at any time. We also taught you how to transform negative thoughts into good ones and look on the bright side of life, which may help you live the life you've always desired. In addition, we discussed how you might use mindfulness to improve your mood and cognitive function. Following that, we looked at strategies to improve your relationships and get rid of those getting in your way and giving you problems. This would significantly reduce your stress levels. We discussed how to decide what is essential to you and create appropriate objectives that will bring you to a better and more satisfying place in the last two chapters. Finally, we covered stress-management methods that you might use in your daily life.

I sincerely hope that this book has aided you in your rehabilitation. It would help if you conquered the habit of worrying in the same way that a recovering addict must overcome their addiction. Only then will you be able to break the chain and cycle that has been keeping you back. I want you to be free so that you and your children can live happily ever after. The pleasure of living without toxic thoughts may help your entire family. The world will be a better place as a result. There is too much negativity in the world, but you can bring about change by wearing a grin and sharing your good energy with others, allowing them to feel the glow that is your pleasure and contentment. Discover your happy place. Arrive and remain there. This should be your everyday objective. Worry less and strive to spend each day with a sense of achievement. "I can do this!" you should be able to say. “Nothing can stop me from accomplishing my life objectives because I am a guy [or woman] with a plan. It'll all work out in the end."

Thank you for taking the time to read this book. I hope that by following the advice in it, you feel empowered to accomplish great things and that you are on the road to recovery and thriving for the rest of your life.

Feedback

Thank you for reading 'How To Heal Toxic Thoughts'. We hope you enjoyed the book? Please now scan the QR code below to leave your feedback.

Claim Your Freebie NOW!

Get Good At Problem Solving

Want to know the secret behind getting good at problem solving? Everyone seems to be able to do it, but you're stuck in the pile of endless to-do lists with little progress.

Ok, so how do I get my FREE book?

EASY! See the next page

Claim Your Freebie NOW

Instructions:

1. Open the camera or the QR reader application on your smartphone.
2. Point your camera at the QR code to scan the QR code.
3. A notification will pop-up on screen.
4. Click on the notification to open the website link

Also By Rachel Stone

How To Remove Negativity From Your Life

Rid yourself forever from the negative thoughts that plague your life with this amazing, life-changing book.

Also By Rachel Stone

Start Being Fearless, Stop Being Scared

Fed up of being scared of the things in life that hold you back? It's time to take control back and start being fearless.

Also By Rachel Stone

Why Living a Simple Life is Better for You

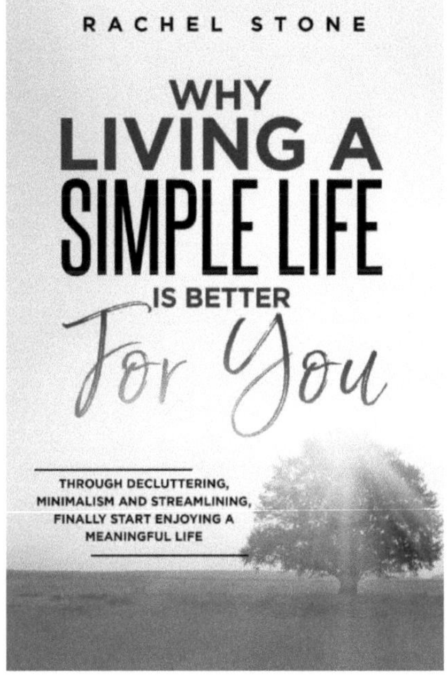

An easy guide to help you change the way you think about your life. Take steps to start living a stress-free life.

Grab the Rachel Stone series NOW

Instructions:

1. Open the camera or the QR reader application on your smartphone.
2. Point your camera at the QR code to scan the QR code.
3. A notification will pop-up on screen.
4. Click on the notification to open the website link

Join in!

If you would like to find out what projects we have on the go, or get in touch with us, simply click on the link below:

http://hackneyandjones.com

9 798215 345115

Printed by Libri Plureos GmbH in Hamburg,
Germany